INVISIBLE GODDESS

Step out
from the shadow
of your divorce
and shine!

Desiree Marie Leedo

BALBOA.
PRESS

A DIVISION OF HAY HOUSE

Foreword

There is something that I've learned along the way, "You can't really take another to a place you haven't gone yourself." Desiree creates a brilliant heart opening invitation to healing and thriving to mend the wounds of a broken heart and battered soul. The personal stories remind us we are not alone on this journey. Invisible Goddess is not simply a book about moving beyond the past but creates an epic opening for all of us to create our strongest life and to never settle for anything less than blissful joy. Each phase of this book will create an unprecedented sense of freedom as Desiree provides the tools and gifts of gratitude to remove the shackles of a broken heart. Invisible Goddess is a book of our time and of the energy and vibration to heal beyond our individual dilemma and moves us towards brilliance beyond our imagination.

This is an amazing book!

Dr. Pat Baccili
(The Award-Winning Dr. Pat Show)
Owner of Transformation Talk Radio & The Transformation Network

Balboa Press books may be ordered through booksellers or by contacting:
Balboa Press
A Division of Hay House
1663 Liberty Drive
Bloomington, IN 47403
www.balboapress.com
1-(877) 407-4847

ISBN: 978-1-4525-7643-5 (sc)
ISBN: 978-1-4525-7644-2 (e)
ISBN: 978-1-4525-7645-9 (hc)
Library of Congress Control Number: 2013911304

Printed in the United States of America.
Balboa Press rev. date: 7/23/2013

For my Mom – my best friend
and my greatest teacher.

To Chris and Andrew – the men who have supported me
through thick and thin; who have shaped and
continue to shape my life.

Contents

Welcome 1

My Journey 3

How to use this book 15

Phase One: Foundations for healing

Chapter 1: Essential self-care 29

Phase Two: Rapid psychological transformation

Chapter 2: Making peace with yourself 67

Chapter 3: The truth of what's emerging........................ 81

Chapter 4: Balancing your mind and emotions.......... 113

Chapter 5: Facing your fears 145

Phase Three: Building your strongest life

Chapter 6: Activating core self-esteem 175

Chapter 7: Re-defining your personal boundaries 209

Chapter 8: The new emerging you............................. 229

Chapter 9: Finding love again 249

Coming Full Circle 259

Welcome

So you're on your own. There's no turning back now. It's over.

I know that heartache, fear, resentment, grief and a sense of powerlessness are only some of the many emotions you may be experiencing right now and so I welcome you with a warm, virtual embrace.

I have walked in your shoes and that's why I am here – to help guide you to awakening those deep, profound areas within that hold the key to unlocking your most meaningful and fulfilled life.

I know that the journey we are about to take together may be challenging for you at times as you take ownership of healing, transforming and empowering every aspect of your life. But I also know what an incredible woman you are. I know how much strength and creativity you have lying dormant in the depths of your being. I know you have the potential for catalysing this life-changing trauma into the type of outcome that you may yet have dreamed of, but not dared to create.

You are not alone. Many women have trodden this path on their journey to greatness. This is the path I now lay before you, the path that we now walk together.

My Journey

Once upon a time, a vivacious young girl grew up in a beautiful sunny city on the coast of South Africa. She lived a wholesome, happy life and much of what made her so happy was her unshakable self-belief. Life was as an adventure and she took challenges in her stride. She also believed in the power of love and, although she thrived in relationships when she became a young woman, she knew that none of them was that special "one" that she felt she was destined for.

In time, this young lady decided to spread her wings as she had always dreamed of travelling the world. She loved engaging with people and she wanted to open herself up to new cultures and new experiences. She saw the world as a giant playground, a place in which one could learn and grow and she couldn't wait to sink her teeth into all that life had to offer.

It was on her travels that she met the one she felt destined to spend the rest of her days with. It was love at first sight and they both knew it. They were soon engaged and married not long after. People that saw them together often commented that theirs was the type of love only found in fairytales. As he was from England, they decided to return for a visit before settling down to a life together on the warm coastal shores back in her home country.

But within a week he was offered a lucrative job with his old company in the vibrant city of London. Our heroine was excited at the prospect of building a new life and a new career in the capital so she postponed the idea of life together on the sunny shores where she had grown up and she consented. She threw herself wholeheartedly into this new experience, embracing the cultural diversity and the challenge of corporate life in the steel towers of some of the most lucrative companies in the world.

She met many fascinating people, with one introduction leading to the next until, eventually, through a series of serendipitous coincidences, she discovered a natural affinity and a deep passion for philosophy, healing and metaphysics. The spark was ignited and, being entrepreneurial by nature, it wasn't long before she decided to pursue a career in complementary medicine. She approached this new venture with a great deal of zest and spent the next few years entrenched in a series of complex courses of study with some of the most renowned teachers and authors from around the world in this field. She felt 'on purpose' and life was good!

But then one day, out of the blue, her husband returned from work and announced that he had been offered a promotion. They would be re-locating to a city called Aberdeen in the Scottish Highlands. A part of her felt unsure about what life would be like on this cold, distant and unfamiliar shore but another part was keen to carve out a new career with all her studies and case studies now firmly behind her. And so she consented.

But life in Aberdeen turned out to be isolating. As a foreigner, she found it hard to break into the tight traditional social circles of the local community and so could not attract the clientele she had hoped. Her husband worked long hours away from home and she often found the solitude overbearing. In an attempt to help, he bought her a sweet little kitten for company. It pacified her for a month or two but kittens don't speak and our heroine loved interacting. She soon felt deflated again. The months rolled by painfully slowly and the days and weeks blurred into one another.

Then one day, quite suddenly, a light appeared at the end of the tunnel. Her husband was offered another promotion that would move them to the cosmopolitan city of Edinburgh. When she saw the beauty that graced this city and felt the warmth of the people, she lit up again and hope returned to her heart. She was pleased for the progress he was making at work and perhaps now, finally, she could get on with her dream of building her own business.

She certainly did. In fact, overnight, she became a success and it wasn't long before her practice was booked weeks in advance. At times she could barely believe she was being paid so well for doing what she loved. The reward of watching the lives of her clients transform spurred her on to ever-greater heights. Life was good again and she felt fulfilled. She made many wonderful and interesting friends. Her husband was also doing well and the years that followed moved them both from one good thing to another. Life seemed close to perfect and she could almost hear the pitter-patter of tiny feet as she thought about this next chapter in their lives.

But her husband was beginning to fly high in his career. After only a few years he was suddenly and unexpectedly offered a major promotion back in London. He would be returning to the city now at the top of his game. Our heroine felt bewildered at the news. She spent days pondering the disruption this would bring to her life, her career and the circle of friends she had created. She had now built up a reputation of her own and was climbing her own ladder of success. She looked around at everything they had built together - their beautiful home, their successful careers, their wonderful friends, their dream life - and she couldn't really believe she was deciding about whether or not to leave it all behind. She wanted to support her husband's career as she had always done but she couldn't seem to escape the burning question that kept gnawing away at her on the inside - "What about what matters to me?" She could not have known then that the sacrifice she was about to make, at this very crossroads, would set her on a path of great despair for many, many years to come.

Our heroine dutifully reasoned that they both needed to be happy in their careers. And he had promised faithfully to support the start-up of her business in London in every way that he could. And so, once again, she consented.

They purchased a new home on the outskirts of London and rented a property while it was being completed. But she began to feel isolated again. She didn't know a soul and she felt impatient that the completion date for their new home was continually being postponed. That dull feeling of depression she had first experienced in Aberdeen slowly returned as she felt more and more out of sync with each passing day. As the months passed, she began to notice how distant her husband of ten years had become.

She made more of an effort to get closer and communicate with him but he pulled away, becoming a closed book. Then, a month before they were due to move into their new home, he encouraged her to visit her family back in South Africa to attend her dad's birthday, but on her own. This was totally out of character for him. Tired and exasperated, she took the next flight.

Seeing her family was exactly what she needed and the sunshine really lifted her spirits. But a week into her visit, after unfamiliarly sparse communication with her husband, he called one day to tell her that he wanted to end their marriage. She didn't think she had heard him properly so she asked him to repeat it. He did. She was speechless. Devastated. She tried to respond but nothing came out of her mouth. In that moment, she felt the bottom of her world and her stomach fall out beneath her. The silence became deafening. It was as if the earth suddenly stopped turning as she watched her dreams shatter into pieces in slow motion in the same family home in which they were dreamed into existence. She jumped with a start as the teacup she had been holding smashed to the floor, snapping her back to the reality of the moment. She didn't understand. He couldn't explain. She hung up the phone and spent the rest of the day in bed, in a state of shock, with the covers pulled securely over her head while her family tried, in vain, to console her.

The next few weeks were a blur. She returned to England and attempted to get to the bottom of what had happened. She moved into their new house on her own, her husband adamantly refusing to join her. Still, he could give her no legitimate reason why he wanted to end their marriage, other than that he didn't want to be married any more. Soon enough though, she discovered that he had met someone else and, although he denied an affair, somehow this new female friend, a psychology student, had confirmed his suspicion that he was not living a fulfilled life within the confines of his marriage. The days dragged on ad infinitum, with her begging for them to attend counselling. He began legal separation proceedings instead. It was over. He was gone. She wondered how they had got here. What had been the turning point? When had the love of her life, turned into this stranger she barely recognised?

She was forced to put their new house on the market and, slowly the finality of her situation began to dawn on her. She had lost everything. A thick black fog descended on her and became her new companion in this strange city. It was an icy February in England that year, she had nobody to talk to other than her family over the phone, thousands of miles away, and she felt completely alone. This was her first real taste of disempowerment. She had failed. She had traded her business, her home, her friends and her lifestyle for the progression of her husband's career, affording him the fulfilment he so craved, and it had cost her everything.

Although our heroine felt paralysed, locking herself away in the weeks that followed, all was not quite lost. One day, she noticed a coffee shop near her local supermarket and decided to go in. She saw the headline on a magazine cover that questioned whether or not self-help books were truly effective in times of crisis and she was suddenly reminded of who she was. She went to the nearest bookstore and purchased as many self-help books on divorce, separation, relationships and self-esteem as she could lay her hands on, promising herself that she would not stop until she found a solution that worked for her - a way to formulate a plan for moving herself out of her state of despair and disempowerment.

She read and read and read, day after day, night after night. But the solution eluded her.

One might think the story ends there - that finally, after selling the home and splitting the assets, she found a way to confront her fears, take up the lesson, empower her life and move forward. But, unbeknown to our heroine, she had not yet hit rock bottom. There was one more devastating twist she would take on this difficult path in her life's journey. One more crucial mistake she would still make before she found her way. And this would serve up even greater despair than she had experienced thus far.

She met a man a couple of months later, a seemingly charming and loving man. Although she felt nowhere near ready to trust in love again, he was patient and extremely nurturing towards her and so she let him in. A strong bond seemed to be forming between them and she breathed in the promise of new love, giving him her trust. She started her business again and things began to improve.

But a couple of months into the relationship, he suddenly became ill. Seriously ill. He developed the type of illness that threatens to take one's life. His family, who lived in Europe and enjoyed extreme wealth, begged her to give up her business and take care of him, as they were so concerned for his life. They promised full support until his recovery and, beyond that, they promised further support for getting her business back on track again.

Another huge crossroads. She felt sick to her stomach. There was so much at stake. She had only just begun getting her life and her career on track and she felt protective of it. But his life was at risk and he had supported her in her own healing process. How could she refuse when he so desperately needed her? So she turned her back on the intuitive voice that told her to walk away, shook hands with reason and consented.

She spent the next two years caring for him at home between a series of hospital visits, nursing him back to health and dealing with the many setbacks in ways that she never imagined she had it within her to do. And at first, she tried to keep her business going alongside the chaos of what soon became everyday life. She felt stressed and exhausted beyond respite. It also took more and more energy to drown out that nagging voice inside that kept telling her to get out.

And then he made a recovery. She felt victorious! They had beaten the odds. Feeling inspired, she turned her focus back to her career and began the task of getting her life back on track, now relying on his family's promise.

But hope was short lived and after only a few weeks his health took a downturn once again. His family, for reasons of their own and completely unexpected, no longer found it convenient for her to live there and asked her to move out. She was numb with shock and utter disbelief. Not long after that, he ended their relationship, not even returning her remaining possessions.

The second taste of betrayal and disempowerment. This time it was overwhelmingly bitter and any shred of remaining innocence dissolved instantaneously as she watched this man that she had given her all to, whose life she had repeatedly saved, disappear practically overnight, refusing to have any contact with her.

You may be wondering at this point if this story has a happy ending. Or perhaps you take the opposite view and think our heroine's behaviour is preposterously self-sacrificial. If you do, I invite you to take a look at the lives of the many women around you who are in relationships. Notice how, in a myriad of subtle and not so subtle ways, many of them are losing themselves bit by bit each day, giving up on their dreams or succumbing to the powerful but subtle expectations of society regarding the roles they should play.

Many of them, like me, and millions of other little girls around the world, were brought up on fairytales of white knights on horses who will whisk them off to their castles where they will live happily ever after. Many of them are placing the needs of their partners and their families before their own, disconnected from their own dreams and desires and disempowering themselves immensely as the years pass by. They think that, because they are doing all the right things, being compliant and making the right kind of sacrifices, they are somehow protected from disaster. The truth is, they are not.

What you have been reading is an exact account of the events of my life. What you have been reading is closer to the reality of how fairytales often end. But, as it turns out, there are gifts in the trauma so allow me to finish my story.

That second relationship ended abruptly right at the beginning of the global recession of 2008 (which hit the UK particularly hard) taking my home, my business and the last bit of financial security I had left. I had barely enough savings to sustain myself long enough to start over. I had no premises from which to continue my business and had been out of the corporate world for ten years - long enough to be totally redundant, especially in an economic climate where people were losing their jobs. I felt I had no choice but to return to my family in South Africa and live with my parents while I tried to figure out what to do next. Of the eight areas of life in which we all engage, I had lost everything in the top five. I felt totally defeated and desperate to understand how to make my life work. As much as I understood the function of the mind-body connection, I had no real and lasting concept of the hidden dynamics of human behaviour. I had no idea that life was calling me to break my addiction to playing small and putting the needs of others before my own. I had no idea that life was calling me to fulfill a destiny far greater than the pain and misery I was experiencing.

All I had left was the love of my family and a burning desire to draw on my twelve years of experience as a coach and alternative health practitioner, so that I could find a solution and set myself free. I knew I needed help fast! And I knew that if I didn't make change quickly, I would reach a point of no return and I would never get back up again. That's what kept me going.

It's amazing when you're down with nothing left to lose, how life will guide you rapidly when you start to pay attention. Or perhaps it's just that you begin to follow guidance for the first time because that's all you have. When the student is ready, the teacher appears and shifts your inner compass. His name was Dr. John Demartini, a well-renowned international philosopher and human behaviour specialist. With perfect timing and divine synchronicity, he turned up to talk in my small hometown. A place he had never visited before and has not visited again since. Knowing he had something important to share with me - the mechanics of which would change my life - I spoke with him after his talk, sharing my background and professional experience. He invited me to become a facilitator of his work. With an innate feeling that I was being fast tracked to a new kind of destiny, I spent the next 18 months training at his institute in South Africa. I went on to facilitate with him at seminars internationally and conducted my own private coaching consultations and workshops, helping hundreds of people in different countries overcome psychological trauma and emotional stress.

In an attempt to move my own life forward, I started to combine all that I had learned and practised over the preceding decade in my work, with some of the cutting-edge techniques that I was learning. The combination became a powerful mix that brought unique and fresh new insights to my life. As I did this, change began to happen fast. Real hope was ignited deep inside my soul and it wasn't long before I started to attract women that had gone through similar experiences to me. They were looking for answers the same way I was. Answers to the question of how to heal, transform and empower their lives after the devastation of broken relationships. Without realising it, I had begun the process of developing my own unique process, the application of which was powerfully propelling my life forward on every level.

I returned to London at the beginning of 2010, emotionally

and psychologically ready to confront the long climb up that mountain of building my life back from zero. Using all of the processes that I had created, and after a monumentally long absence, I broke through the last fragments of fear and back into the corporate world in London, still steeped in an economic recession. I secured stable income and kept my coaching business going on the side.

With each small success, more of my confidence and my spirit returned. And a new vision began to emerge – a desire to share my story with women and guide those who wished to take that same journey from dependence to independence after divorce or separation and create meaningful, self-fulfilled lives. To share with women the hard-earned secrets of how to take ownership of every area of their lives in a way that gives them back to themselves - in a way that ensures that they would never want to part with it again.

I had learned the very hard way that when we give up the power to create our own lives we are doomed to a life which others are forced to create for us. And we are never truly free. When we have nothing to offer a relationship, other than an expectation of loyalty in exchange for the inner or outer things we choose to sacrifice, the relationship is always doomed.

Of all of the many good books I read when I was going through my experiences, I wish there had been one like this available to me for the guidance I so desperately sought. I have walked in your shoes, I know your deepest hurts, your regrets, and your greatest fears. I understand the emotional paralysis you're feeling. But I also know the purposeful road that lies ahead of you should you choose to answer the call to connect with yourself at the deepest level and create a more meaningful life. And I promise you that some day soon, when you look back, you will be in awe of who you have become. And you will thank that higher power that brings order and balance to life, for having reached out to you from across the cosmos, through the entire grand organised design of life, and called YOU to a higher purpose. Called you to become more. That day you will know you are truly blessed.

My deepest hope is that this work will guide you to embrace your highest potential, remind you of the truth of your essence and inspire you in your becoming, as you welcome in the new life that awaits you. That you will take full ownership of yourself as the powerful and creative being that you are and that your will and your courage will guide you. That you will create all the love, beauty and power in your world that you so rightly deserve and that, eventually, you will pass this knowledge on to your daughters. I will hold your hand through this entire journey and I hold you lovingly in my heart.

Desiree

x

How to use this book

In my practise I usually facilitate all the steps in this book (and more) over a period of 6 weeks. However, I have chosen to present the material here in a way that is flexible and allows you to work through the process at your own pace. This is because you will find some parts easy while other parts will require a great deal more self-reflection and you, as the reader, will need to decide when you are ready to move from one step to the next. The material in this book is designed to bring about meaningful and lasting change so please don't rush through it, rather work at a pace that feels right for you.

You will find the tools in this book very practical and I will guide you throughout on how to apply them, with care and awareness, so that you quickly begin to experience powerful results. As we go along you will soon begin to see that these tools can be re-used throughout your life at any stage to recover from a crisis or to re-direct your life at any turn.

My process consists of three phases which are reflected in this book as follows:

Phase One – Foundations For Healing

We start by addressing the initial shock and emotional trauma stages that follow a big breakup. This phase relates directly to your *physical* healing. It will help you transcend the *Reptilian Brain* thinking process (which is activated in response to stress and trauma). This is the part of the brain that perceives that you are under threat and puts you in "fight or flight" mode, causing chemical imbalance in the body which you experience as numbness, shock, heartache, insomnia, etc. The exercises in this part of the book help bring about internal balance, preparing the way for clearer thinking so that you can move onto the next phase of the process – psychological transformation. This occurs at the next level of the brain – the *mid-brain*.

Phase Two – Rapid Psychological Transformation

Now we are ready to address the mental perceptions that cause the emotional turmoil after the breakup. This phase relates directly to your *mental/emotional* healing and will balance your perception of events, transcending the *mid-brain* thinking process (concerned with everyday thoughts, emotions, senses and perceptions). Once we are able to put intense emotions, resentments and fears into perspective and create balance on this level, we pave the way for the next phase of the process – emerging an inspired new life. This occurs at the next level of the brain - the more evolved *humanitarian brain*.

The Triune Brain of consciousness

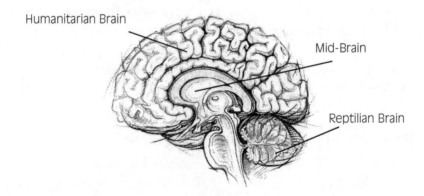

Humanitarian Brain

Mid-Brain

Reptilian Brain

Phase Three – Building Your Strongest Life

Finally, we introduce steps for planning and implementing the new life that you wish to emerge. This phase relates directly to your *spiritual* healing and will allow you to activate a new vision for your life from the more evolved and inspired *humanitarian brain*. It assists you in bringing about profound inner and outer transformation, putting you back in the driver's seat so that you can re-direct your life to meet this new vision.

 Reflections and Healing Action Steps

There are pauses for *Reflection* as well as *Healing Action Steps* throughout the book, both are vital components of the process and it's essential that you complete each one before moving on to the next. For this purpose, I recommend that you locate or purchase the following:

• 1 entirely blank notebook (for working through these exercises).

Additionally, for working through the first Phase of the book, you will also require:

• 2 entirely blank notebooks, preferably with different covers and with cover designs that uplift or inspire you (the purpose of each notebook will be explained during that part of the process).

As you work through the book, I ask one important thing - that you bear with the process. The sequence is there for a reason, and as you move through the chapters you will realise why this sequence makes perfect sense. Please trust the structure and follow the format.

Throughout the book you will also read stories, all of which are real examples, drawn from my years of working with many brave women who wanted to reach out for help and improve their lives. I have changed their names in order to protect their privacy.

For the sake of reference, and because I predominantly work with women who have come out of relationships with men, I refer to "her", "he" and "she" in a way that may seem stereotypical at times but I assure you that, no matter who you are (man or woman) or who you have been in a relationship with (male or female), if your partner has walked out on you and you are devastated, the tried and trusted methods in this book can really help make a difference to your healing process.

Are you ready to get started? I know I am...

Phase One

FOUNDATIONS FOR HEALING

What I want you to know, as we embark on this journey of healing and transformation, is that you are going to be just fine. In fact, you'll be more than fine. Like thousands of other women around the world who have felt exactly the way you do right now, you will come through this and, if you commit to your healing and do what is necessary to transform and empower your life on every level, you truly will bring about a profound personal transformation. You will be stronger, wiser and in a much greater position to positively and powerfully impact your life, your future and the lives of those around you.

Going through a major life transition as a result of divorce or separation, especially if it was your partner's decision to leave and not yours, brings up a monumental amount of mental, emotional and physical stress that can leave you feeling traumatized, leading to long term emotional scarring if not deal with properly. Suddenly, your entire world is thrown into chaos. The words you never expected to hear uttered from the person you love and trust, are now a reality. Suddenly you're unsure about who you are and how to live life on your own. You can't seem to make sense of anything, you feel out of sorts and you are faced with all kinds of unimaginable new scenarios. Intense feelings of anger, betrayal and fear, in particular, have gripped you as the familiar foundations beneath your feet disintegrate into dust. You feel lost and helpless, as if you've fallen down a black hole and nobody can see you or hear your inner screams, even though there may be copious amounts of people rallying around you, offering their support. You feel invisible and, even if someone were to come along right now with the perfect life jacket, you're not entirely sure you would recognise it or have the strength to hold on. Please understand that these feelings are all perfectly normal. They are part of the psychological stages that accompany a relationship that ended this way.

As much as I know that you desperately want life to be able to carry on just as it always has and you keep thinking you'll wake up from this horrible dream - the truth of the matter is that, from now on, your life will never look the same again. And this is your point of power, whether it feels that way or not. That is the fact and the reality that I want you to embrace right now. Because accepting that is the first step on your path to healing.

What's happening on the inside

It's important to understand what's happening inside your body at a time like this. If you don't, you will mistakenly think that you have no control over the feelings of heartache and depression that have taken hold. As you lose the safety of the foundations on which your life has been built for so long, you also lose your psychological grounding and enter into a mild state of psychological shock and denial. Your body responds by adjusting its internal chemistry in an attempt to protect you but this protection mechanism, if left unchecked, can quickly become unhealthy. Regaining a sense of wellbeing requires that you actively participate in restoring some type of balance that helps you cope because the body is not designed to handle this type of psychological stress reaction long term.

The good news is that there is much you can do to restore your internal balance - we will cover this in depth in the next chapter. But first, let's look at the internal chemical responses you are having to the emotions that dominate during the initial stages of a breakup.

Your internal chemical response

The rollercoaster of shock, fluctuating emotion and fear that results from your reaction to all this overwhelming change, puts you in a state of heightened sensitivity. With life as you know it now under threat, your brain's thinking and response processes divert away from the higher, more evolved parts (from which you function when you feel safe, happy and content) to the lower more primitive "fight or flight" parts (associated with survival and self-defence). This primitive response is there for one reason – to protect you in a crisis. However, when this part of the brain starts to run the show, clear thinking goes out the window and feelings of fear, survival and revenge dominate. This, in turn, sets off a potent stress response within the body, releasing a cocktail of stress hormones, which flood the system and induce hormonal changes that keep you in a high state of alert, preparing you for danger and enabling rapid response. Emotional fluctuations, heartache and insomnia result.

Reflections:

Are you aware of your ability to think clearly going out the window?

I hope that in some way it reassures you to know that this is your primitive brain stepping in to protect you!

To put things into perspective, much of what affects you at this initial stage of your breakup stems from fear – those exaggerated "what if" scenarios that run through your mind and are largely related to "worst case scenarios". You are not really in imminent danger of death. You are not really running to escape being hunted by a wild animal. Yet, as you perceive what you are experiencing with a great intensity of despair and fear, these are the signals that your brain is receiving and causing your physiology to react accordingly.

When you are in an extreme state of emotional distress, the limbic system (the part of your brain predominantly associated with emotion) becomes over-stimulated and responds by

flooding the appropriate stress hormones to prepare you for fight or flight. Your brain does not know the difference between what is real and what is imagined, it only responds to signals received.

In this state, hormones like nor-epinephrine, epinephrine and cortisol are released into your bloodstream and work together to increase heart contractions, trigger the release of glucose from energy stores within the body and increase blood flow to the muscles. At the same time, immune function is put on hold, blood is drawn away from the skin and the reproductive areas and diverted to the muscles to prepare them for action. All processes relating to growth and repair within the cells are temporarily shut down so as to deal with the immediate crisis.

Never underestimate the powerful impact that emotions have on the internal mechanics of the body. In my years spent working as a holistic practitioner, I repeatedly witnessed how emotions like worry, fear and self-doubt can literally eat you up from the inside. In the long-term, a trauma situation like divorce or separation, where you remain in a highly stressed or shock induced state for a long period of time, can cause your body to progressively lose its ability to maintain homeostasis and a host of physical ailments may begin to manifest, such as:

❀ Insomnia.

❀ High blood pressure.

❀ Lacklustre skin and hair or hair loss.

❀ Spots or acne breakouts on the skin.

❀ Effects on metabolic processes leading to weight loss or weight gain.

❀ Stomach ulcers.

❀ Changes in the menstrual cycle.

Worse still, if emotions from trauma are suppressed, they can collect in the tissues of the body for decades exacerbating all sorts of conditions later in life.

Reflections:

Is your body showing you signs of stress?

What distinct changes have you noticed?

Transcending the "fight or flight" response

The good news is that you can counteract these stress reactions and allow yourself an easier transition during this time. The earlier this is introduced, the smoother the transition.

Once you lift yourself out of the symptomatic "fight or flight" stress stage, you will feel more balanced and better able to restore mental clarity. This opens the doorway for you to begin the deeper psychological work of processing and releasing events where it really matters - on the mental and emotional levels. This is where the true cause of the chaos originates and, equally, where the real power for healing and transformation, ultimately lies.

On a subtle level, it is the combination of your perceptions and emotions that set these chemical reactions off in the first place. It's what you're seeing, believing, remembering and imagining that causes the body to induce a response to those signals. But when you are in the centre of experiencing these stress reactions and you begin to lose your sense of balance, it actually appears the other way around – as if the stress hormones in your body are solely responsible for causing you to think and feel the way you do.

Jennifer's Story...

Jennifer was in an absolute state when her marriage of 8 years broke up. The first few weeks were a blur. She frequently disappeared into a dream world and was losing stretches of time staring into space, thinking of nothing in particular. She stopped eating regularly and couldn't commit to her usual routine. She found herself lying awake at night, unable to cope with the reality of what was happening in her life. She would wake up exhausted and have to take regular naps throughout the day in order to function. Her heart felt as if it had been ripped out of her chest and the tiniest reminder of what she felt she had lost would send her into long episodes of inconsolable sobbing. While Jennifer knew that she was having a somewhat natural response to the major loss she was experiencing, she realised that her "foggy" head made it almost impossible for her to think rationally in any way. It was only once she took control of her diet, introduced some daily walking in a beautiful park nearby and sought help from a registered homeopath that she started to feel calmer and more able to cope. Well-meaning friends had suggested she go for counselling, however Jennifer knew that, at this stage, she was too fragile mentally and the thought of having to process anything was simply too overwhelming.

When changes in life occur suddenly, it's a natural response to react from a place of fear - as if your very existence is under threat – because in many ways it really feels like it is. But it's that very perception that sets the ball of internal chaos rolling and creates a vicious cycle of imbalance between the intricately connected network of thoughts, emotions and chemical reactions. Once this system becomes distorted, it creates a negative impact on your rate of recovery.

To balance your body's internal chemistry, your emotions must move into balance. And for your emotions to move into balance, your perception of what is occurring must first move into balance as well.

This book addresses transformation on all three levels – physical, psychological and spiritual. But in order to clear the path to the psychological work, it is critical to introduce essential daily self-care activities that will help balance your internal chemistry, enabling you to think and feel more clearly. This will ground you, help you build healthy new foundations and, most importantly, get you out of the primitive stress areas of your brain. You will then be better able to address what's happening with a calm, more rational frame of mind.

Let's dive right into creating your daily Essential Self-Care routine.

Chapter 1

Essential
Self–Care

"No problem can be solved from the same level at which it
was created."

— *Albert Einstein* —

In order to balance the rollercoaster of thoughts and emotions
that you're now experiencing, it is essential to introduce effective self-care steps that you can implement on a daily basis
to bring your mind, emotions and, consequently, your hormonal
reactions into a more balanced state. This is the most important
commitment you will make towards your healing.

This chapter will guide you through setting up a self-care routine and provide you with tools that help ensure you stick to it. If
you're reading this with doubts about how you will find the time
to make this work, or you're thinking that you may be tempted
to not follow through on this part of the book and just skip past
it, then I invite you to consider how you can honestly connect
with the inner power required to transform the rest of your life

without these solid foundations. The better question to ask your-self is: what will happen if I *don't* make the time for these steps?

These Essential Self-Care steps are also highly transformative tools that can be applied again after any future traumatic event. They are a new way of approaching life that you can easily adapt in the years to come as you continue to grow.

Before we begin

People generally treat us the way we allow them to and the way we treat ourselves. The more you value and prioritise yourself, the more others will value, respect and prioritise you.

In a later chapter in this book we will talk more about person-al boundaries but at this point, as you begin to put Essential Self-Care into practise, what is important is that you protect the new space you are creating for yourself. If your divorce or separation is not going particularly amicably and upsetting phone calls or communications are causing major distress, then you may need to put a little distance between yourself and your availability and/ or response times. This does not mean that you hold up impor-tant discussions, legal matters or any other urgent family matters, but it does mean that you deal with them at times of the day that are more suited to you and during which you feel more centred and in control. Your self-care is an absolute priority and you should not allow people or events to disrupt your new routine. You may find this difficult at first, as you begin the process of changing a lifetime of unhealthy habits towards yourself, but you must persevere because if there was ever a time in your life to put yourself first – this is it!

The 10 steps of Essential Self-Care

In a weird and bizarrely wonderful way, it is with thanks to my background in the field of natural therapies, combined with the intense anxiety and depression I experienced after the breakup of my own marriage, that I present these ten little gems to you. They were born of a powerful mix of knowledge and quiet desperation.

In my darkest hours, I quickly realised that nobody was coming to rescue me and that I had to become responsible for my own healing process. By responsible I mean response-able, that is "able to respond" to what was occurring. Nobody could give that to me or do that for me. I realised that when I made self-nurturing my priority and committed to ensuring that I followed these steps every day before I even attempted to take on anything else, then healing would begin to occur at a remarkable rate. I have since imparted these steps to others who have undergone depression resulting from crisis and those who made the same personal commitment enjoyed great results too.

I encourage you to put these Essential Self-Care steps in place, as soon as possible. In my practise I usually introduce a new step each day while ensuring that the preceding steps continue to be practised.

Let's get started.

Step 1: Clean up your diet

The number one priority for you right now is to take control of your diet and nutritional needs and introduce regular, healthy eating and hydration. I know that the temptation is to either stop eating or be over-indulging in comfort foods that offer temporary emotional relief. Both will ultimately wreak havoc on your internal chemistry and your emotional state.

Please make the commitment to starting a healthy eating routine immediately, even if you can't see how this is high on your list of priorities. I promise that it will give you new stores of energy to draw from and you will reap a multitude of benefits on many levels.

Eating foods that have zero nutritional value will exacerbate the effect of the cocktail of stress hormones already moving through your system. Caffeine, processed foods, sweets, pastries, crisps and fizzy drinks should all be avoided right now. They will only leave you feeling low in energy, unable to concentrate and induce headaches. They give you that "foggy" head or "hangover" feeling, and will also contribute to feelings of lethargy and insomnia.

On the other hand, a nutritious and well-balanced eating plan will help reduce food cravings, increase energy levels, relieve insomnia, bring greater clarity to your thoughts and help stabilise your emotions. Superfoods, high in antioxidants, will also boost and protect your weakened immune system.

Healthful and nutritious foods to include in your diet are:

- At least six glasses of well filtered or bottled water each day. Hydration alone will help flush the toxins from your body and clear your thoughts.

- A variety of fruit and vegetables. These are high in antioxidants and will protect you by keeping your immune system strong.

- Green foods (like spinach, broccoli and kale) that also contain high levels of antioxidants but have the added benefits of helping to balance the metabolism.

- Healthy soups and salads (like vegetable, minestrone, carrot and broccoli).

- Lean protein (like fish, chicken and beef - organic where possible). These are good sources of protein and iron.

- Complex carbohydrates (like wholegrain bread and cereals, brown rice, lentils, potatoes and beans). These are slow release carbohydrates that keep you fuller for longer. They are nutritious and also initiate the release of seratonin (the "feel good" hormone) into your system.

Foods that contribute to emotional and physical chaos and should be eliminated from your diet for the moment are:

❀ All forms of refined sugar (like sweets, chocolates and biscuits). They cause your blood sugar levels to spike, giving you a false high which induces temporary emotional relief but causes you to crash a few hours later, leaving you feeling worse than you did before. This sets up a vicious cycle of cravings, emotional guilt and unhealthy eating patterns. Just say no!

❀ Junk food (like crisps, pastries and cakes) that are loaded with sugar, salt and saturated fat. They may be great "comfort foods" but they contain very little nutrition and exacerbate the emotional rollercoaster. Consuming these types of foods can very quickly pull you into an addictive cycle and contribute to feelings of self-loathing.

❀ Excessive caffeine (like coffee, Coca-Cola, Red Bull, chocolate). This exacerbates the already high levels of cortisol in your blood stream and will contribute to insomnia. Stick to one cup of coffee and tea a day if you must, preferably try to consume calming herbal teas that contain cinnamon, chamomile and fruit extracts, especially in the evenings.

Some women lose a lot of weight at this time, which, over a long period, can have a negative impact on their bone density and metabolism. Other women begin comfort eating and gain a lot of weight, often in an unconscious attempt to be unattractive to men so that they don't have to suffer hurt again.

If you have lost your appetite and are losing weight (like I did when my marriage was breaking up), then the key is to focus on giving your body as much nourishment as possible to keep your energy levels up and prevent your immune system from crashing. Focus on eating small portions of healthy food a couple of times throughout the day rather than eating nothing at all. Eat six to eight times a day, even if a portion only consists of a piece of fruit or a handful of nuts - don't skip any of your mini-meals. Make sure that you're eating enough protein and carbohydrates and drinking enough water and don't be tempted to replace a small meal with a bar of chocolate or packet of crisps – these are pointless choices that rob you of sustained energy in the long run. Also, it would be best to avoid caffeine altogether as it will further surpress your appetite.

If you are emotionally over-eating, the chances are you're throwing in a lot of excess carbohydrates, sugary, salty and fatty foods. Immediately start cutting down on all junk food and try to keep it out of the home altogether. If you've increased your normal daily intake of food then cut your food portions down into smaller portions and eat more frequently. Increase your intake of water (even if you have to drink it with some type of cordial until you get used to it!). Most importantly you need to begin to substitute the sugary and fatty emotional food fillers with seeds and nuts, plenty of fruit, salad and protein. Complex carbohydrates like whole grains, wild rice, brown rice, soup and vegetables and oats are excellent substitutes – they sustain blood sugar levels and help you feel fuller for longer. They will also help you feel more positive.

If you are finding it particularly challenging to eat well, I encourage you to get some support from a qualified nutritionist or think of someone in your social circle who is knowledgeable in this area - I cannot emphasize enough how important this is.

Resist the temptation to use alcohol or any type of recreational drug as a means of escape from the way you are feeling. Alcohol is a depressant and will combine with the stress hormones in your body to take you into an even deeper state of emotional chaos while recreational drugs will leave you feeling mentally paranoid, depleted and far less able to cope with your current circumstances.

Although I am not a doctor or fully trained nutritional therapist, I assure you that making these changes can make a big difference. I have many friends and associates in this field that I regularly confer with and they have helped many of my clients who made the commitment to follow through on them.

There are also supplements that can assist at a time like this. The following are merely guidelines - please consult your doctor, pharmacist or nutritional therapist to ensure that they are suited to your general state of health before taking them and ensure that you choose a reputable brand:

❀ A multi-vitamin and mineral supplement.

❀ An essential fatty acid supplement, combining omega 3, 6 and 9 in the right ratios, which can help keep your hormones balanced.

❀ High quality fish oils, as they can often assist in counteracting depression.

Remember that your health is your responsibility. If you feel you would like a more personalised approach to your health, I highly recommend you consult with a nutritionist. Additionally there are also many good books available on this topic.

Reflections:

Which foods can you introduce into your diet today to help build strength and give you added energy?

Which foods are robbing you of vitality and need to be eliminated?

How will you ensure that you stay well hydrated?

Step 2: Ditch insomnia

It can feel absolutely torturous if you are losing sleep due to stress and anxiety over a long period of time. If you're suffering with severe insomnia, as many people going through a divorce or separation inevitably do, you may need to consult your doctor. A course of sleeping pills can be helpful but they can also be highly addictive so do discuss the best option with your doctor and opt for the milder forms that take you through more natural sleep cycles where possible. These will leave you feeling less groggy and more alert in general.

If you feel you would like to try a more natural approach, complementary therapies can also provide helpful solutions at a time like this. In my years spent working as a holistic health practitioner, I eased many people through times of crisis with therapies like reflexology and aromatherapy and it was fascinating to see how well the body responded to these.

Reflexology, massage, aromatherapy and homeopathy can all be very useful for calming the mind and emotions, thereby promoting restful sleep. Their effects are mostly immediate and they contain no adverse effects. However, if you are pregnant please check with a qualified practitioner as some of these remedies may not be safe.

Aromatherapy – lavender and geranium calm and balance the emotions while frankincense is excellent for relieving a sense of loss. You can also plug in an aromatherapy hot stone and safely burn lavender throughout the night to aid with restful sleep.

Homeopathy (including flower remedies like Bach Remedies) – Rescue Remedy is well known and available over the counter – its particularly useful for helping with shock. Walnut promotes emotional adaptability in times of change, while protecting from outside influences.

Massage and Reflexology – are both excellent therapies that aid in the healing process. They help soothe and balance mind, body and emotions. They are touch therapies and therefore have a nurturing effect. They help dissolve stress and tension and induce calming hormones. They also leave you with a continued awareness of relaxation and are helpful in alleviating insomnia, anxiety and hormonal imbalance. You may need to commit to weekly session for six to eight weeks but I honestly can't recommend this option enough.

If you are serious about counteracting emotional stress and nurturing yourself through the divorce process, I recommend you find a reputable accredited Reflexologist, Massage Therapist, Aromatherapist or Homeopath who you can trust and can visit on a regular basis as you transition through this phase of your journey.

Ultimately though, in order to alleviate insomnia altogether, you will need to resolve the contributing underlying psychological factors with a professional - someone who can counsel and coach you through unresolved issues.

Reflections:

What steps can you take today towards ensuring you get a better night's sleep?

Will you try the natural route or the allopathic route, or both?

When will you take the first step and get help?

Step 3: Breathe for balance

So few people truly understand the powerful and calming effect that deep breathing has on the entire nervous system. When we are stressed or afraid, breathing becomes irregular and shallow and less oxygen is able to circulate and reach the cells of the body. Practising deep breathing at least twice a day can have a profound effect on calming the nervous system, delivering more oxygen to the cells and improving general circulation. This can be done anywhere and anytime of the day – in toilet breaks at work, in the car or even on the train. Ideally you should aim to do this exercise three to four times each day, preferably at three to four hour intervals:

❀ Close your eyes and breathe in slowly to the count of seven.

❀ Hold for a count of seven and then breathe out slowly to the count of seven (or beyond if required) until all the breath is expelled.

❀ Repeat the entire cycle five to seven times.

❀ Try to keep a rhythm going as you count.

Once you have completed this exercise you should feel more calm and centred. You will probably notice that mentally you feel a little clearer and less overwhelmed.

If something particularly stressful happens, like having a distressing phone conversation and you need an immediate and effective return to balance, the following exercise can very quickly ease distress by balancing the left and right sides of the brain:

❀ Close your eyes and focus on your heartbeat.

❀ Close your right nostril with your thumb and breathe in through your left nostril, slowly to the count of seven.

❀ Hold for a count of seven and breathe out for a count of seven.

❀ Now release your right nostril and close your left nostril.

❀ Repeat the exercise, breathing in through the right nostril slowly to the count of seven, holding for a count of seven and releasing for the count of seven.

❀ Continue alternating between nostrils until you feel calm and centred (usually at least three rounds with each nostril).

Reflections:

Where and when can you break from your daily routine to practise some deep breathing?

Can you set a reminder on your mobile phone or somewhere else that prompts you to do this at least 3 times a day?

Step 4: Movement and Creation Statements

Moving your body in the form of some type of exercise every day is an invaluable way to kick-start those elusive feel-good hormones. And combining this movement with some well chosen statements that affirm your healing process and the new direction you want your life to take, gives you a positive new focus to take into your day. I like to call these Creation Statements. When combined with exercise they become a powerful duo that can bring re-assurance and help induce feelings of well-being. With focus, they can also help bring about total transformation in any area you choose to develop.

Movement

The first part of this step is to introduce a way to move your body daily and to ensure that this is special time spent with yourself that you look forward to and don't see as a chore. It's nurturing time. As much as you may be feeling tired and lethargic at the moment, taking twenty to thirty minutes of daily exercise is absolutely essential for you right now. This doesn't have to be an extreme move like joining a gym, it simply requires that you spend time moving your body every day to release the toxic emotions that are building up in your tissues. Exercise also releases endorphins into your system, which profoundly counteracts stress hormones.

E-motion is Energy in motion and can be effectively released by expending energy (through movement). We all know that in any given moment, your body language directly reflects your state of mind and, likewise, you can alter your state of mind by altering your body language. When you feel depressed, your entire body takes on a slumped position, reflecting your attitude. If you were to pull back your shoulders, stand tall, head held high, put a smile on your face and walk around like that for a little while, you would find that soon you will feel a little uplifted. Remember that the mind, the emotions and the body are intricately and powerfully connected and they are all instrumental in assisting each other to restore equilibrium.

The most ideal activity that I can suggest is brisk walking somewhere beautiful in nature because it has the added meditative benefit of helping you feel more connected. Research has long shown the positive effects that being out in nature has on the psychology of human beings. By walking, I mean walking at a fast pace, moving your arms and shoulders and twisting slightly at the waist. Walking around your neighbourhood while paying attention to the flowers and trees along the way, can be just as useful. If you live somewhere that makes it impossible to walk near nature or if you prefer a vigorous workout at the gym or taking up a spinning class, that's perfect too. These types of cardiovascular activities can be especially beneficial if you are holding onto a lot of anger that needs releasing.

But the key is that you move your body *everyday*. Whether you simply dance vigorously to your favourite music at home (choose songs that remind you of times in your life when you were happy and felt invincible), do some yoga postures, play tennis, cycle or run up and down the many stairs in your home with mindfulness! This is *your* time to connect with *yourself* and start a new routine of spending time nurturing *yourself*. You will enjoy the emotional release and after a few days you will probably notice that you are also sleeping better and have a greater feeling of well-being. This is a daily practise that I would encourage for life because once you start to see the benefits, you will most likely want to extend the time that you spend engaged in this activity each day.

Reflections:

What form of movement can you introduce today so that you can start to access those feel-good hormones?

What time of the day can you consistently commit to doing this?

Creation Statements

A Creation Statement is a meaningful positive affirmation, something you repeat over and over to yourself with conviction. For example,

I now choose to heal and create a meaningful future

Undoubtedly, they can feel a little fake at first but I highly encourage you to persevere. Say them like you mean them, even if

you don't at first. After some repetition you will begin to build an emotional connection to them, an important ingredient for amplifying their effect. Practise in the mirror and look into your eyes as you say them so you can get the momentum going. Notice what it feels like to say a statement half heartedly, and what it feels like to say it with conviction, as if it were already true. Within a few days you will begin to believe these statements and within a few weeks you will begin magnetising their effects into your life as if by magic, so persevere.

When you first work with Creation Statements, please keep them simple! Many people mistakenly think that churning out long, complicated declarations that address their deepest fears, hopes and dreams across paragraphs and pages are empowering. But it's really not possible to hold the feeling all the way through a long declaration like that.

Start with one or two of the following simple creation statements:

Today I relax and allow life to nurture me.

**Life supports me in all that I do, I am
safe and I have all that I need.**

**Everyday, in every way,
I become stronger and stronger.**

Creation Statements can also be introduced during your daily exercise routine. They allow you to create a new way of thinking about your life and open many doorways. Where the thought goes, the energy flows.

Choose one creation statement per day or work with the same one for as long as you need to. Continue to affirm your statement throughout your exercise routine and take it into your day from there, repeating it as a mantra as many times as you can.

Once you have been practising this for a while and you are feeling the results, I recommend you formulate your own creation statements. Write some that are specifically meaningful to you. It's important to keep them in the present tense, as though whatever it is you desire has *already* happened. So, instead of saying something like "I want financial abundance", say "I am financially abundant in every way".

Change your creation statements whenever you like and re-write new ones when you feel ready. Most importantly, they need to become a daily practice and you need to commit to keeping them going! For maximum effect and to really begin to shift your focus, each creation statement should ideally be repeated continuously throughout the day, both mentally and out loud when possible.

Even if you can't relate to doing this at first, just do it anyway. Do it until you can feel every cell of your body slowly getting on board. Trust me, if done properly this really does work. Change the statement each week as you make progress but, preferably, work with one statement at a time using no more than two statements a day until you feel ready to take on more.

Here are some examples of creation statements that can help:

People love and support me wherever I go.

Everyday in every way I am becoming more empowered.

**I nurture myself and accept love as my
natural state of being.**

**I am powerfully healing my life and creating
a new life that I love.**

Life supports me through this transition bringing me all that I need for my highest good and I am safe.

I hold all the power needed to change my life.

I now choose thoughts and beliefs that lead to freedom.

I open my mind and my heart to the best possible outcomes for me.

I love and approve of myself just as I am.

I am worthy of love in every moment.

These Creation Statements will become a part of the way you think from now on and will positively impact the way you feel. They will help pave the way forward, bringing new people and experiences that match their intention, into your life. As the momentum increases, so will the opportunities that you attract, until you are surrounded with all the love, beauty and inspiration that you desire.

Reflections:

What is it that you feel you need most right now? Write your own creation statement (affirming that need as though it has already been met) and introduce it into your daily exercise routine.

Step 5: Channel and release your emotions

In addition to using exercise to release the physical build-up of emotions, it's important to release the psychological build-up as well. You're most likely feeling angry, betrayed and afraid much of the time and it's inevitable that you will engage in mental arguments at various times of the day. The unfortunate thing is, this is like taking small daily doses of poison and hoping that someone else to die. Nobody is affected but you and you are hurting yourself immensely each time you do this. It's important to find a constructive outlet for all the mental and emotional ranting that you need to release during this time of major transition.

Emotional journaling

Emotions are symptoms and not causes. That's why getting professional help in a situation like this is vital, because until you expand the way you are perceiving events, you will be stuck on an emotional rollercoaster, the stress of which can take years off your life!

When releasing negative emotions, remember that:

- Ultimately, they will need to be dealt with at the source, otherwise they start to build up again (a bit like a kettle that boils, lets off steam, switches off and then slowly builds up to boiling point again).

- The only way to effectively dissolve emotion is to be able to bring your perceptions to a balanced state.

- Writing your emotions down in a journal everyday not only helps release them but can also produce helpful new insights.

- Daily journaling combined with regular exercise can be a very powerful emotional outlet.

The reason that journaling is so effective is that it allows you to express and release a wider range of emotion, including fear, which can lead to the expression of hope and, ultimately, even compassion. Releasing emotion through journaling requires that you operate from the higher brain states. It brings insight and resolution along with release and can invoke spontaneous answers to some of the fundamental questions you're asking right now, like, "why is this happening to me?", "how could he do this to me?", "what do I do now?", etc.

When my marriage broke up I went to all sorts of workshops that had me beating pillows and yelling out my anger along with other angry participants in the room. And doing this for more than 30 minutes in one session definitely will connect you to a very primal anger (associated with the lower, more primitive levels of the brain) that triggers the awareness of all sorts of other compacted past events that have angered you! While it feels great to get this type of raw anger out, I found that it left me feeling physically drained with a massive headache and cost me a few days of downtime afterwards getting my energy levels back up. While I think these techniques can be helpful to some degree, this method is really just a temporary band-aid of relief that feels good until the mental arguments start kicking in and building up more emotion again. Why? Because none of what you are feeling is being dealt with at the fundamental level of perception. If your perception around an event were balanced, there would be no predominantly negative emotion that accompanies it.

If you do need to release pent-up anger and want to beat a pillow or have a good scream alone in your car while you're driving every now and then, absolutely do it (provided there is no risk to you or anyone else on the road)! It's healthy to express yourself, particularly if you're feeling depressed. Being able to express anger from the lethargic depths of depression is actually a healthy sign that you are moving towards healing as it is often precedes taking action. But do this in addition to daily journaling.

Working with a skilled professional who can ask the types of questions that swiftly help you to make sense of your situation can assist you in revealing the deeper meaning behind events and help you dissolve painful emotions.

Divorce and Separation is an opportunity to re-examine multiple aspects of your life so it's important to enable emotions to flow consistently instead of disconnecting from them or stuffing them down with a myriad of distractions. If emotions are not released constructively, you will find yourself lying awake at night when there is nothing else to occupy your mind, in floods of tears as the ever-expanding emotional pressure valve begs for release. Long term, if left un-dealt with, this can lead to health issues.

Reflections:

 How many times a day are you having mental arguments with your ex and any others involved in the situation?

Wouldn't it feel great if you could get it all down on paper, off your chest, and really have your say without any restrictions?

How to do emotional journaling

Choose one of the notebooks you set aside as described at the start of this book (How to use this book). Label this as your "Emotional Journal" and be sure to dedicate it exclusively to this purpose. Use it to write down what you are feeling or experiencing everyday. If you feel really stuck initially, try not to think too much about what you are writing. If you're finding it difficult to write anything at all, then write "I am finding this exercise difficult" and "why I'm finding it difficult is because…" and just keep going until it all starts coming out.

Nobody will be reading your journal except you so there is no need to censor your writing. Use this opportunity to let it all out! Here are some examples of themes you can work with that will help you constructively channel your emotions:

a. Write your breakup story – your thoughts and feelings about what is happening.

b. Write a letter to your ex telling him everything you have not been able to say up to now. Write exactly how you feel, un-censored and give your emotions free reign, regardless of what comes out or how dark it is.

c. Write a letter to any other people that may be involved in your situation and say everything that you need to say. Get it all off your chest, totally uncensored.

d. Write down your fears for the future, what the worst-case sce-nario would be if they were to come true and how you would deal with those worst-case scenarios.

e. Write a letter to your ex thanking him for the life you lived together and listing all the things you gained from the part-nership. This is a letter of gratitude and should come from a place within that is genuinely felt in your heart when you are ready.

f. Write about your hopes and dreams for the new life ahead of you.

Choose a time of day where you know you have at least twenty minutes to spare so that you can easily get into a healthy habit. Be sure to vent every emotion, get out all your frustrations, jus-tifications and self-sacrificial resentments. Keep venting, even from the darkest place inside of you, until you feel ready to move to the next step of channelling your feelings more constructively. But you must get to the point where you move on from simply ranting - steps (a) to (d) above - and begin to write letters of thanks and inspiration - steps (e) and (f) above. Take your time without wallowing. If you find you are stuck on a particular step, speak to someone in your support network (we will soon be setting this up with people you can trust).

If you continue doing this daily you will be amazed at how much you will get off your chest and how many helpful insights will open up to further guide you on your path of healing. Once you have completed your healing process you can use this activity to begin mapping out the vision for your new life. Set goals and daily actions for the things you want to achieve in each area (more about how to do this in a later chapter). As you reach your goals and continue on your journey, you can evolve your plans and set higher goals - all from this simple platform of focusing for twenty minutes a day!

Reflections:

What time of the day can you set aside to consistently allow yourself 20 minutes for emotional journaling?

When will you complete your first journal entry?

Step 6: Practise gratitude

Gratitude is one of the most powerful healing forces we have to work with. It may sound strange to be thinking about practicing gratitude at a time like this but I assure you this is the perfect time to begin.

When I first separated from my husband it was my wise mother who kept telling me to find things to be grateful for. I found this incredibly difficult because I felt so resentful and I literally had to start by being grateful for the most obvious things, like the roof over my head and the food on my plate.

One night, frustrated, in tears and unable to think of anything else in my physical life to be grateful for, I turned to my health. When I was done giving sincere gratitude for every part of my body that still functioned properly, I was, again, at a total loss.

In despair, I began crying, begging the universe to show me how to be truly grateful for things because I just couldn't feel any of it. And then I turned my attention to myself.

I realized, from the truth of my heart, that I was incredibly grateful for my kindness, my sincerity and my warmth. I was grateful for my ability to feel so deeply and for the part of me that contains such great wisdom. I was grateful for the gifts of insight that have guided me so well throughout my life. For my work and my ability to be able to take on this powerful life transforming journey. And when I really started to get it, the tears of desperation turned to real tears of self-appreciation. By the time I was three weeks into it I was tempted to call up my ex and thank him right there for the opportunity of helping me discover all the amazing stuff I was excavating deep within myself - things I felt truly grateful for.

No matter how dark a place you feel you are in, take time every morning or night, preferably before going to bed, and write down at least five things that you are grateful for. Attempt to grow this list with one new item each day. The list does not need to look the same each day. Review your day and find things to be grateful for. If you have had a particularly bad day, take a moment to search for the good things that happened that you may have missed because of the way you were feeling or look at some of the positives that will result from the bad things that happened. You may just surprise yourself. Either way, pretty soon you will see that life really is on your side.

Your relationship treasures

An important exercise to complete on your path to healing is to be able to identify the treasures you have gained from your marriage or long-term relationship. As part of your gratitude journaling, it's important to identify all the ways in which your relationship contributed to the different areas of your life as well as to the person that you have become.

Make a list of all the gifts that the relationship brought into your life as well as how your life has been enriched by having participated in the relationship. If it helps, you can write a list like this for your ex as well, from your own perspective, particularly if you're feeling unappreciated. Write down all the ways that your ex's life was enriched by knowing you and then add this additional appreciation of yourself to your list of gratitude.

Gratitude is the most powerful tool we have at our disposal for healing. When we focus on appreciating the things we do have everyday, they tend to grow. Try not to do this from a place of fear or revert to negative gratitude's like "thank you that I am not as bad as this person" or "thank you that I don't have to put up with X anymore" - that's not gratitude, it's judgement and criticism and will bring completely the opposite results!

True heartfelt gratitude will harvest great gifts and promote feelings of love, balance and wellbeing. When you're ready, take this practise out into your everyday life and watch the magic start to happen.

Reflections:

What are the most profound ways that your life has changed for the better because of the years spent with your ex?

Will you consistently set aside 10 minutes for gratitude journaling in the morning or in the evening? When will you complete your first journal entry?

Step 7: Create your support network

Now that you have placed yourself in a healing cocoon of Essential Self-Care, it's time to look at ways to set up your environment in a way that best supports your healing. One of the most important things you can do right now is to create a support network of people you can trust to help you transition through this period. The following guidelines will walk you through the process of identifying key people to surround yourself with. The goal is to set a positive framework of support that can help you navigate the stormy waters and offer the right type of nurturing and objectivity when required.

You are not alone

First and foremost, remember that you are not alone in what you are going through. Right now, as you're reading this, there are literally thousands of women out there going through exactly the same feelings of despair as you are and some of them are in situations so dire that they don't even have the financial resources to be to purchase a self-help book.

Any sense of loss will leave you feeling frightened, vulnerable, isolated and incredibly lonely on the inside, particularly if you're one of those people who shut down to the help of others when things aren't going well in your life. Please remember, no matter who you are or what you are going through in your current circumstances, you are not alone in this and there are many other wonderful people out there who will understand and help you. This is not the time to turn your back on those around you or isolate yourself. Reach out to the people that are good for you, be yourself and let them know what you need.

Look around your social and family life for one or two people that you can approach and ask to buddy up with at this time. Please, please, please, do not share your intimate thoughts, hurts and feelings with those you feel you cannot trust or bear your soul to anyone who does not have the natural sensitivity and skill to be able to support and encourage you in the right way. This will only leave you feeling more confused.

The best friends are those who have emotional intelligence and will calmly listen, allowing you to find your own answers and supporting you when needed instead of imposing their own rigid ideas and beliefs onto you and becoming irritable if you don't follow through on their advice. A good friend will also be able to sit with you in silence at times, if it's just company that you need, and encourage you to take a break from expressing hurts and fears when appropriate by introducing fun social activities.

Refrain from trying to counteract feelings of low esteem by going out "on the pull" with your friends at all cost. *Drinking too much and letting other men chat you up or take you home in an attempt to feel desirable or to get revenge on your ex will only knock your self-esteem further because you will only create more drama that you'll need to work through.* The kind of self-esteem you are about to create cannot be found anywhere outside of you.

Jumping prematurely into another relationship from a desperate need for emotional support or a desire to feel loved is also another no-no! There are many wonderful men out there but there are also many men who will take advantage of this situation and it will not end well for you! Allow yourself the opportunity to heal ethically and build a strong inner foundation for a more empowered future and you will use this event for what it was meant – an opportunity to transform your life into something more fulfilling and engaging. Otherwise, all you're doing is creating more baggage to be dealt with in your next relationship. A relationship that is not built on a healthy beginning rarely goes the distance.

Reflections:

Who do you trust right now and who springs to mind as a healthy support for you in all the right ways?

When will you make contact with them?

Dealing with the reactions of others

People around you will react to you in a variety of ways at this time – some will try to smother you with care while others will avoid you like the plague. Neither are particularly helpful so it may be best, where possible, to avoid both. When people over-care for you or try to wrap you up in cotton wool, it robs you of your ability to connect with your own inner guidance and can often promote abdication of responsibility. Meanwhile others, who pretend to care while clearly avoiding you as much as possible, can hook you into a disempowering loop of feeling unacceptable or ostracised because of the way your life is changing.

If you find yourself in the position where some of your friends or family members suddenly don't want to spend time with you, try not to take it personally. It's not that they don't love you or that they don't want to be there for you. Understand that for them to help you deal with what's happening in your life right now, they would have to confront their own deepest fear - that what's happening to you may someday happen to them.

On the other end of the scale, be wary of spending too much time with people who have gone through a similar experience somewhere in their past from which they have not fully recovered and still carry deep emotional wounds. The last thing you need right now is to start engaging in "woundology" sessions, comparing and validating each others' emotional scars. This will only keep you stuck!

The same applies to family members or friends who never particularly liked or got on with your partner in the past and are now using your break-up to justify their opinions of his character flaws. They will consistently put your partner down in an attempt to justify their judgements and to reassure you that you are better off now. Repeatedly indulging in these types of conversations for lengthy periods of time may bring about temporary gratification but, ultimately, they will leave you feeling worse, saddling you with guilt and confusion in your quiet moments. Trust me, as tempting as it is, putting someone else down to make yourself feel better will take you in the opposite direction to where you need to go, so limit these types of conversations or cut them out altogether. It's far healthier to express your emotions constructively with an objective professional, appointed support buddy or in your journal instead.

Reflections:

Who do you recognise as an unhealthy support to be avoided at this time?

How will you begin to limit the content of your conversations with this person?

Joining support groups

While there are many organisations out there that run support groups for divorced and separated men and women, I am not a fan of most of them. Too often participants sit around in these groups, re-visiting their stories over and over again, ingraining their misperceptions of events deeper and deeper into their psyches to the approval and cheers of other participants. They become more and more numb until, eventually, they convince themselves that the indifference they feel has brought about healing.

Many of these groups also delve into a host of past issues in an attempt for participants to identify areas in which they need to "fix" themselves, further perpetuating the distorted perception that the divorcee is somehow "flawed". Divorce is an event, not a condition. Please understand that I fully appreciate the difficult circumstances associated with some divorces, particularly when abuse and infidelity are evident, but these types of groups, although sometimes temporarily useful in the initial stages of expressing how we feel and speaking up about what we need, are often dependency based and not truly equipped to move you beyond your pain into a whole, independent and inspired place.

Step 8: Clear out your space

It's time to clear out the space around you so that you can connect back to your own personal identity and deepen your practise of self-nurturing.

You should now feel ready to pack away everything around the house that evokes memories about your ex. While I understand that you have spent years, even decades, building a home and a life together and that it's not possible to empty out an entire house, it is important to put away special items that serve as a daily reminder to the life you shared. This includes any items like ornaments, trinkets, wall photo's, photo albums and other items of endearment that may be lying around the home making you feel sad each time you look at them.

For now, I want you to box them all up and pack them away. Please do not throw them away - the aim is not to remove them right now, it's simply to put them out of sight. The time will come when you can get them all out again and go through each item, less emotionally charged and ready to decide what is best kept and best to let go of.

Make sure that none of your ex's clothes are hanging in the cupboard. Return them immediately or box them up to return later. Also ensure that none of his books or business/technology items are lying around as reminders. If you are not on speaking terms, drop them off with a friend or family member who can pass them on.

If at all possible, introduce immediate changes to your intimate space - areas like the bedroom and the bathroom. Buy new bed covers and curtains or introduce wall paintings, candles and other ornaments that nurture you and reflect your individual personality. Buy candles and bath salts for the bathroom and change the towels. Put as much of your own stamp on your personal space as you can and place your Creation Statements where you can easily see them and feel inspired when you look at them. Bring a music system into your bedroom and buy soft healing music and meditations to calm you.

It's also a great idea to box up or throw out and replace all of your underwear and sleepwear. If this is not possible, at least be sure to get rid of anything that he may have purchased for you and replace the rest, bit by bit, when you can.

It's best to complete this entire exercise in one swoop on the same day. Clearing your space is an essential step to creating a self-nurturing new environment in which you can begin to create an independent life with your own energy.

Reflections:

What small thing can you introduce into your personal space that reflects who you are, makes you smile and connects you back to your own identity?

What do you need to return to your ex and what needs boxing up?

When will you commit to completing this exercise?

Step 9: Get clear on finances

I have seen so many women whose partners walk out on them face sleepless, anxiety filled nights because of the issue of finance. Some men can be particularly cruel, especially if they are in control of the purse strings. They withhold information and financial support from their partners in an attempt to control the terms of the divorce or separation. Remember, generally speaking, by the time a man is walking out on a relationship, he already has near enough one hundred percent closure on it (even if he says he hasn't) and has most likely already sought legal advice regarding his financial position.

When my marriage broke up, I was in a similar situation. I had just completed a major re-location with my husband to progress his career and when he left, a couple of weeks after the move, I was financially completely dependent on him and in the dark as to what would happen to me. I assumed that the assets would be split down the middle which, at the time, would have left me with barely anything. Funny enough it was an acquaintance, not a close friend, who strongly encouraged me to seek legal advice. I resisted for weeks because a small part of me felt that if I did seek advice, I was acknowledging that the relationship was over and I found this difficult to accept at the time given, especially given that the relationship had ended so suddenly.

But once I became aware of my legal position, the power dramatically shifted into my lap and I realized I was in a far stronger position to negotiate than I had previously thought. Not only did understanding my rights bring tremendous relief, it also helped me feel stronger and enabled me to make self-empowering decisions. If you are in a similar position, this is often one of the most empowering steps forward that you can take. Don't hesitate, just do it.

Once you know your financial position, take action and create a budget for the coming months, along with an action plan for getting back to work if necessary. Allow yourself a small cocoon of time before starting back at work if you feel you need to, and then go about putting your action plan into place. Start organizing the activities you plan to embark on - getting back to work, moving home, etc. and take control! Nothing stops fear and anxiety in its tracks as effectively as setting achievable goals and taking action. Ask a friend or family member that you can trust to help you and hold you accountable to your new action plan.

Reflections:

Do you know where you stand financially after your divorce or separation?

If not, how will you get clarity on your financial situation and when will you do this?

What steps do you need to take to gain back your financial independence without interfering with legal proceedings?

Step 10: Lock down your day

Although this is the final step of Essential Self-Care, it is definitely one of the most powerful! Locking down your day means that you live in the present moment as much as possible. It means that you establish a mindset of living only from the moment you wake up to the moment you go to sleep. You do not dwell on the pain of yesterday and you do not indulge the fear of tomorrow. Just one day is all there is in your world right now – today. And don't forget to breathe!

If you think about it, the past and the future really don't exist, except as memories and probabilities. Your point of power is in the present and it's what you think, feel and do in *this* moment that creates the next moment.

Locking down your day means that you do not allow yourself to focus on the hurt of the past or indulge the fear of the future outside of your emotional journaling (there you can freely focus on the past and the future as a means of expressing yourself as a whole). The reason for this is to limit the time spent fixating on negativity throughout your day and to focus only on con-structive activities. If you find your mind wandering to negative past or future scenarios, bring your attention back to the present with your chosen Creation Statements or create new ones to help counteract the negativity that's distracting you.

The truth is that most of the things we remember from the past are always slanted towards our own ideas, values and filters and are, therefore, never the whole truth. And the same goes for the things we worry about in the future, most of which never actually come true.

Locking down your day looks something like this:

❀ Waking up and getting on with your daily routine (including organizing the kids, any social activities, work and so on) with your attention and focus 100% on the activity you are doing.

❀ Eating well, drinking good water and taking quality multi-vitamin and mineral supplements as well as drawing on complementary remedies, if desired, to help maintain emotional balance throughout the day.

❀ Using the Essential Self-Care steps for releasing and expressing emotions through Exercise, Creation Statements and Emotional Journaling.

❀ Drawing on your support system and breath-work as needed.

❀ Going to bed with a heart of gratitude (gratitude journal).

If you commit to these steps everyday, while spending as little energy as possible indulging your "yesterdays" and "tomorrows", you will not only rapidly transform your life, but also establish powerful and lasting routines that will benefit you physically, mentally, emotionally and spiritually for the rest of your life.

Reflections:

Where will you place a reminder to lock down your day where you can see it throughout the day (e.g. set an hourly reminder on your mobile phone)?

What can you use as a talisman (a piece of jewellery or special item, like a crystal) that you can carry with you as a reminder to lock down your day?

Congratulations, you have now established real and meaningful steps to creating profound personal change. As soon as you have firmly established your Essential Self-Care routine, continue on to the next phase of the book where we'll get started on bringing about profound psychological transformation.

Phase Two

RAPID PSYCHOLOGICAL TRANSFORMATION

Welcome to the second part of the journey. Now that you are well on your way to achieving physical balance through Essential Self-Care, the next step is to focus on reaching psychological balance. Achieving this will enable you to open the door to real and lasting transformation. This is essential before embarking on the final phase of our journey – re-creating your inner and outer life.

Your choice to heal

Going through a divorce or separating from a long-term relationship, particularly if it was your partner who decided to walk out, is undoubtedly one of the most challenging and heartbreaking situations you can encounter in life. But it also plants a seed of potential for one of the greatest opportunities you will ever be given to re-discover yourself and embark on a journey of profound personal transformation. It is an invitation to create an exceptional new life and become the woman you were always meant to be, the woman you may have been denying for far too long.

The shock of hearing your husband or partner say that they no longer want to be with you is devastating, especially if it is sudden and unexpected. In an instant, the firm foundations beneath your feet, to which you have grown so accustomed, become quicksand and you feel yourself sinking, fast.

Even if you reached the point of divorce through the slow decay of a dysfunctional long-term relationship that did not involve any shock factor, you still face major change and you will value this part of the process in helping you take stock of each area of your life.

While the physical, emotional and mental impact of what is happening is enough to drive you into a state of deep despair, most damaging of all are the distorted conclusions that you'll formulate at this time about who you are in the face of your deepest fears and rapidly changing circumstances. Then you'll carry these distortions into your future relationships as facts, resulting in the creation of deep emotional scars.

Worse still are the ways in which these distorted conclusions, however subtle and unconscious, can gradually influence your children who are learning to deal with life situations through the example you set, particularly your daughters, who are also learning how to become women.

I believe that there are a distinct set of recovery solutions for women whose partners have walked out on them and that, in order to make a complete recovery, it's essential to move through these stages in the right order. However, so many women fail to do this and carry tremendous pain for years, even decades, quietly living powerless lives of desperation and creating unnecessary ill health in their bodies.

Global statistics show that 50 percent of first marriages end in divorce. But shockingly, 63 percent of second marriages and a staggering 74 percent of third marriages fail as well. It's time to make a decision. Right now. Are you willing to do whatever it takes to move forward? This process is not a band aid. It's not a quick, easy fix. It takes courage to self-reflect to these depths and it requires great commitment but the rewards are lasting.

Reflections:

 Ask yourself honestly – would you like to take this pain and heartache into your future, processing it along the way in a series of failed relationships? Or would you prefer to confront it and free yourself right now?

In the next chapter we will begin the process of balancing the mind and the emotions. We will focus on healing every area of your life as you spiral out of the divorce and separation process. For this reason, it's important that you commit to completing the exercises at the end of each chapter, applying them to your own life and circumstances. So let's begin.

Chapter 2

Making Peace
with Yourself

"Make peace with yourself - with the deeper part of you that wants this experience. Therein lies your true power for transformation."

— Desiree Marie Leedo —

I believe that divorce and separation, along with every other type of trauma, including the loss of a loved one through death, is the most powerful catalyst for profound personal evolution that exists in life. I know, first hand, how infuriated and resentful we feel towards our partners when they are walking out the door, especially in the face of all that we have invested and sacrificed within the relationship. But what we often can't see and don't realize in the heat of it all, are the many unseen opportunities and gifts that are offered to us on a golden platter in that moment.

I believe that if you take the necessary steps to heal, ask the appropriate questions, allow yourself to put the event (and who you are now becoming as a result of it) into perspective, confront your fear of the future, create an action plan for success and take the necessary steps to bring about the right kind of change, all the while walking confidently into your future with your self-esteem and personal boundaries intact and your head held high - you will have come a long way in using the trauma of divorce for exactly that which it was soulfully intended – the greatest opportunity to answer the call to creating a more meaningful, self-fulfilled and engaged life. This becomes a gift for you to pass on to your family, friends and children, enriching their lives by positively impacting their ability to transform their own future life traumas, through your own example.

Why is this happening to me?

One of the first questions we ask when confronted with divorce is - why is this happening to me? This chapter is designed for you to begin answering that question as best as possible within the framework of this book.

If you look back over the last couple of months, or even years, you'll notice that, for some time now, your life has felt different. You may only have had a very subtle sense of this but you've been quietly aware that, at times, you're asking yourself questions, wondering, or even daydreaming, about ways in which you wish your life could be different.

Maybe you've felt a little dissatisfied with the way your life is going or the mundane routine that you seem to be living. Or you've been thinking about things that used to be an important part of the person you once were - things that no longer seem achievable anymore. Or you've wondered about areas of your life that you would like to change or empower in order to feel more whole and connected.

You've wondered, in your quieter moments, if the way you're living is all there is to life. You've thought about talents, personal or professional, that you engaged in the past, that now appear to be going to waste. Or dreams you've been putting on the back burner because the day-to-day demands of family life take up so much of your energy and you're waiting for the "right moment" to get back on track with them. Or, perhaps you've even been playing out some "what if" scenarios about your relationship, some coming from a place of fear and others from a place that wants more for your life.

These thoughts, ponderings, daydreams and musings have all formed part of a deeper soul-searching, they are micro moments that have led up to this one. And you're not the only one whose been doing it, your ex has been doing it too.

And suddenly, here you are. Facing a divorce that you think you didn't want. You're dealing with the loss of your partner, your lover, your best friend. Your life has been turned completely upside down. You're really afraid about what the future holds and all you want to do is negotiate your way to sanity, even if it means giving up everything you value and making sacrifices for the rest of your life, just to put the relationship back together. Yet you feel yourself falling deeper and deeper into a black hole. You're drifting into numbness, moving around on auto-pilot and lacking anything that resembles enthusiasm or even hope for the future.

Step away from the abyss!

While I fully appreciate the length and breadth of the emotions you're experiencing and I know that there are deep, dark corners within yourself that need to be excavated, I also want to remind you of the need to do this constructively so as to prevent you from a long downward spiral that may cause you to associate the bottom of the pit with your new reality.

Let me share with you, right now, the science of creation in the hope that it will remind you to keep some of your energy in positive territories. Through my research in the field of Quantum Physics, I've really come to love and appreciate the complex intricacies of how waves and particles behave. How they literally wrap themselves around our beliefs, thoughts and emotions, moulding them, over a period of time, into manifestations of reality. But this mechanism operates on one cornerstone alone – *that reality is magnetised on the outside to directly reflect the way energy is arranged on the inside.*

So how does energy get "arranged" on the inside? Your personal energy matrix is a powerful thing that can make or break you so you need to understand how to begin working with it. What do I mean by personal energy matrix? This is a collection of things about you that make up your energy signature, which gently pulsates out into the world around you, communicating everything about you, without you saying a word. It's a collection of your thoughts, emotions, beliefs, the tone of your voice, the way you move your body, how you express yourself and your innermost dominant beliefs. Everyone has an energy signature, sending out waves that vibrate at a frequency particular to that person. And as your energy pulsates out from you, it magnetizes people, events and circumstances that match its frequency, directly towards you. When you first meet someone, it's the way both your energy signatures interact as you engage that gives each of you an initial impression and feeling about whether or not you like each other. This happens instantly, deeply and somewhat unconsciously, usually in around five seconds flat. What your energies communicate in this short space of time, are whether the two frequencies (yours and theirs) actually 'gel' or 'click' as a match and whether or not you can trust this person.

Much like you can't actually see the act of a flower or a tree growing from moment to moment, you also cannot see how, moment to moment, your innermost dominant thoughts, beliefs and emotions are magnetizing people, circumstances and events that match it, on the outside. If you allow yourself to remain in despair more than 50 percent of the time, chances are you will begin to attract all sorts of doom and gloom and then mistakenly think that this is how your life will be from now on.

Your personal energy matrix is also constantly shaping your future. When you feel depressed and the world seems like the darkest place, you attract people and events that reflect that darkness back at you. When you feel inspired and in the flow, your energetic vibrations increase in frequency, and life just flows much more smoothly. When you have a low self-image and feel victimized, you attract people and events to substantiate that. When you feel strong, capable and able to handle what comes your way, that energy magnetizes people and events to substantiate that. Whatever your dominant frequency, over time, that becomes your reality. It becomes your truth. No matter who you are, or what you have experienced in the past, you do have the choice and the power to change it.

Choose your reality

So, how do you change your reality? By changing your mind, literally.

The reality that you face today is always built upon yesterday's thoughts, emotions and beliefs. All the questions, daydreams and pondering about scenarios that have occupied time and space in your mind over the last couple of months or years, are big clues as to the unconscious dominant thoughts and desires that have so powerfully contributed to bringing you to this vey moment today.

Who you are today is very different to who you were a couple of months ago, let alone a couple of years ago, even if you haven't really been paying attention. And who you will be tomorrow is borne out of the very experiences, beliefs and attitudes you are engaged in today. For this reason we cannot go through an experience like divorce and draw the ultimate conclusion that "time will heal all wounds". Time won't heal anything. Spend some time in conversation with a woman of any age who went through a divorce even decades ago, and you will hear her say things like "oh, that was a long time ago, I'm fine now" or "oh it all worked out in the end, I married someone else so it was a happy ending". Press her a little harder with some probing questions and it won't be long before her eyes glaze over and you witness the evidence of hurt, abandonment and betrayal that's still sitting right there in her energy, as if it happened yesterday. Lead her a little deeper into the conversation and soon you will discover the unique self-protective coping mechanisms that she set in place after the divorce for navigating her life around the mass of unresolved emotional scar tissue that sits wrapped around the distorted conclusions she established to protect herself in future relationships. All to ensure that she made safer choices so that she would never have to endure that kind of pain again.

In reaching for this book you have made the decision not to be one of these women. You have made the decision to take the necessary steps to heal the pain, confront the fear and build your strongest life.

Reflections:

 Can you think of times (good or bad) when you have been feeling a particular way and have drawn in people and situations that matched how you felt?

Your first steps to finding peace

In order to take the first step towards becoming whole again, you need to connect and make peace with the part of you that wanted this breakup. Please understand that I am not advocating that you *consciously* wanted the breakup or that you purposely did something to instigate it. I'm talking more about the greater, unconscious part of you that knows the plan for your life and recognises your true potential and talents. It's also the part of you that understands that your relationship has become a disempowering crutch. That you have lost your connection to yourself and to your own power and that you are indulging in unhealthy habits of co-dependency. That the life you are living, and the lack of self-belief that accompanies it, is no longer aligned with your highest purpose. That you are moulding your identity around someone else's idea of who you are, or should be. This part of you wants you to break out of all of that and into alignment with what you're truly capable of.

I can't tell you how many clients walk through my door and, when I introduce this first step of getting to know and make peace with the part of them that wants the split, they immediately start resisting and debating this profusely with me. They say things like "No I don't want this, I didn't leave him, he left me!" or "Why would I want the breakup of my family?" or "Are you joking? I don't want this? How will I survive financially?" Yes I think I have about heard it all.

But once we start looking at the bigger picture - their frustrations, their lack of self-connection, their unrealised dreams, and the profound ways in which they know their lives will change for the better now that the relationship has ended, I am yet to find a person who doesn't say "wow, yes I can see the part of me that actually wanted this". And they actually begin to feel excited by it. They become curious about their lives again and many even begin to feel a little grateful that their partners walked out at this point because they finally admit that there is no way they would have rocked the boat or left on their own. Life was just too comfortable.

Stephanie's Story...

Stephanie booked an appointment with me a week after her husband of eleven years announced that their marriage was over. He refused to go for counselling. The night before she came to see me, she called to say that her husband had just confessed to multiple affairs throughout their marriage, the most recent being three weeks earlier. She was devastated and felt unsure about whether to keep her appointment with me because, emotionally, she felt so raw. I knew that the sooner I worked with her after this devastating news, the faster I would get her to a place of thanking him for his behaviour so I suggested she keep her appointment and sleep on it, with an option to cancel in the morning.

The fear and upset in Stephanie's eyes when she turned up the next day was palpable. She looked utterly defeated with shoulders slouched on both sides of her pale and gaunt face. She could barely speak and, when she did, I quickly realised that she had her husband so high up on a pedestal, I wasn't sure we would really be able to get him down from there. We spent almost half of the five-hour session working on this first step of the process. Stephanie found it difficult to let go. She had been so afraid to connect with all the things she wanted for her own life because she had put her husband right in the centre of it and then wrapped her world around him. She was hanging on for dear life, but when she finally did let go that morning, the results were astounding.

When she switched her focus to other areas of her life, she saw what she was losing out on. She remembered how much she loved her job and loved to travel. She had always dreamt of combining the two but felt afraid that traveling away from home would have a negative affect on their relationship. She started to see that she was living half a life in which she was fulfilling every need her husband had but wasn't allowing her own needs to be met, never mind fulfilled. This sacrifice had made her feel inwardly resentful which impacted her marriage in many subtle ways and also contributed to an inner resentment towards her husband for daring to leave her and go out and get the life that he wanted. She realised she was angry with herself, more than with him. And by the time we had finished looking at how all the things she adored about her partner had been stunting her own growth as a person and how they kept her life neatly revolving around his, she woke up and realised that she had been hiding from the world and from herself. She saw that he was setting her free to answer an inner calling that she had, for too long, been denying.

The change in Stephanie after our five-hour consultation was stag-

gering. She transformed from a slightly hunched and fearful middle-aged woman to a woman with absolute clarity and self-control, right before my eyes. She went home and stopped begging her husband to stay. She took back her self-esteem. She moved out immediately and went on a cruise by herself to reflect on the next stage of her life. This was a big step for her because in the past she had felt socially inept, hiding in her husband's shadow at every social event. She met some wonderful people on that cruise, re-enforcing the realisation from her session that she had excellent communication skills, particularly in social circles with people who shared her interests. This was a far cry from her husband's professional social engagements where the conversation was usually focused on technical knowledge of the industry, leaving her feeling like a wallflower.

In the weeks that followed, Stephanie continued to do the inner and outer work, looking at what she wanted to achieve in every area of her life. She emerged from the experience a changed woman with new friends and opportunities. Nine months later, she stepped into a new relationship that gave her the energy and the space she needed to live her life in a way that was meaningful to her and in which she felt powerfully connected for the first time.

Reflections:

Does Stephanie's story resonate with you in any way?

In which areas of your life have you felt uneasy because you knew you were not living your full potential?

Finding your divorce gifts

Transforming the chaos of your situation into a meaningful new life that you love requires a great deal of insight, courage, responsibility (being response-able) and action.

Soon we'll embark on a powerful exercise that will get you started on the road to transforming your perceptions about your breakup. This requires that you ask yourself, in great detail, how your life will be better as a result of the divorce or separation. But first, here's how Ada found her own answers.

Ada's story

Ada is a holistic health practitioner who came to see me after her marriage of 15 years broke up. When I took her through this step in the process she quickly noticed a pattern around being free to pursue her work without judgement and criticism from her husband and being more available to her clients outside of normal working hours, including weekends when the majority of people required her services. When I questioned Ada further, I discovered that she had always wanted to partner up with other practitioners and create a health centre that offered a variety of complementary therapy services to clients. While her husband had always said he supported her work, he was often critical of her "holistic beliefs". He expected her to be available to him and the family in the evenings and on weekends. He would become angry and upset when she wanted to participate in weekend talks and seminars to expand her client base and made subtle remarks that left her feeling guilty for not prioritising family life.

While Ada was terrified of what the future now held for her financially, especially as she was trading their beautiful, big family home for a small apartment, when we looked at the timing of their breakup, she acknowledged that, had they not broken up now, they would definitely be breaking up at some point in the future. There were too many other issues popping up that were holding her back from living the fulfilled life she sought. Another decade on, a break up like this would be financially crippling for her and, most likely, have prevented her from achieving her goals at all. Ada saw that this was the perfect opportunity to throw herself wholeheartedly into doing well with her work and realizing her dream of creating the holistic centre she had envisaged. At this stage of the process Ada became teary with deep appreciation towards her partner for setting her free. As we continued to work through the next steps of the process, for the first time she became supremely confident about her future and felt she didn't want to waste another moment.

Healing Action Step

How will your life be better because of this divorce or separation?

This may seem like a simple question, but the insights you will gain from the answers you provide are profound and complex.

This step of the process is designed for you to genuinely realise the gifts that await you following the end of your relationship so you can wake up to the full potential of where your life is now headed. This will get you feeling excited, take you out of the passenger seat and put you back in the driver's seat of your life. My clients usually finish this part of the process buzzing with new found confidence and looking forward to the next step.

To complete this exercise, you'll need to work in your notebook, across several clean pages that provide you with enough space to develop your thoughts.

Take the following into consideration as you think through your answers to the question. It may be helpful to refer back to these as often as you need to while working through this exercise:

• **Take your time:** You will need to spend an hour or two finding your own answers to this one question.

You can list these out as bullets or numbered items using as many pages in your notebook as you need. It may help to remember that your mind is designed to come up with the answer to any question that you ask, no matter how long it takes. If necessary, sleep on it and take a day or two to think about your answers. Pay attention to your dreams and allow new insights to unfold.

• **Start by asking yourself the obvious:** List the ways that you have already recognised that your life will be better without your ex. Here you can have a bit of a rant and put down all the things that frustrated you, no matter how petty – all the things that annoyed you that you will be pleased to be done with (like the toilet seat!)

• **Then, put away your list of ranting (above):** Start a new page and take things a step further. Introduce at least seventy new bullet points and fill them up by looking into all the different areas of your life. Identify a myriad of meaningful ways in which your life will be better from now on because of your breakup. Look at your friends and family, interests and hobbies, your social life, your finances, your relationship with yourself, associations and affiliations, your health and vitality, your career goals and other general life goals, interests and dreams. Somewhere there are some huge hidden gems, waiting to be discovered.

• **At this stage, avoid the temptation to give negative answers like:** "I won't have to put up with his arrogant behaviour anymore" or "I'll be better off without his controlling ways". You can do this in the first part (when you are ranting) but if you find yourself doing this now, PLEASE STOP! This is not an opportunity for character assassination, rather, it's an opportunity to look forward and explore new horizons.

- **A real benefit would be to identify ways in which you've been liberated as well as areas of your life you wish to re-engage:** These are areas that have become stagnant or stunted by all the time and energy you chose to invest into your relationship instead of yourself. This may include your relations with others, the attainment of long held dreams, aspects of yourself that you want to nurture or develop and activities that you love to engage in.

- **Allow the hidden truths to emerge:** I need you to keep looking, until all the unconscious and hidden truths begin to emerge in recurring patterns, while you focus on being as non-repetitive as possible. This will unveil the unconscious and subtle motives to the part of you that actually wants this to happen. Keep looking until the lights start going on inside you. It may help to look at some of your answers and again ask yourself, "How does this answer lead specifically to my life being better?" In this way you can find answers within answers. Keep going and you will access the deeper layers that contain the deeper insights.

- **Perfect timing:** Once you have provided seventy answers, ask yourself how this is the perfect timing in your life for this event to have occurred, based on the answers you provided in the previous question? Imagine the breakup happening ten or twenty years into the future. How would you have coped then? Is the timing an act of grace in any area of your life?

- **Persevere:** Remember to keep the fear aside (for now) as we will deal with that in a later chapter. Keep answering this question until you begin to feel enthusiasm about the different gifts that are sitting right in the middle of all the grief. You're now looking inwardly at ways in which you can independently grow and direct your own life. Yes, this new direction may well take time to gain momentum but that's okay. What's a couple of months or even years in the space of your entire life? Remember, where you are now is just a snapshot!

Even though I'm not there to guide you through this exercise in person, I encourage you to courageously complete this process. I say again, it's important that you don't allow any fear to creep into this exercise. If you're genuinely afraid because you have to go back to work and you haven't worked in many years, but you know deep inside that going back to work is the right thing for you because it will bring new friends and interests, then that's a positive! If you feel powerless and dependent and you fear the journey to becoming whole, connected and empowered again but you know intuitively that this is the right path for you, that's also a positive. Set the fear aside and answer from a place of truth. We will get to the fear and the "how to" in detail later on.

Next comes the exciting step of discovering how you can clear the decks and create space for all the gifts you've just discovered. Are you ready to identify and integrate the many facets of your life as a woman and learn how to hold power in each of these areas? Let's jump straight in!

Chapter 3

The Truth of What's Emerging

"The journey of your life will demand that you master every area contained within it. You may choose to do this consciously, through self-governance, or unconsciously, by inviting events to govern you."

— Desiree Marie Leedo —

When I first came across some of the information that I am about to share in this chapter, it was one of the most revolutionary moments of my life. Suddenly, the missing piece of the puzzle fell into place and, for the first time ever, I fully understood why my life just hadn't been working the way I wanted it to.

When the Wheel of Life was introduced to me by Dr. John Demartini, I was absolutely blown away by the realisation of how positively this knowledge could impact the direction of our lives and the lives of those we touch. I still wonder why we aren't taught this in our education systems because I feel it is so relevant to our journey through life.

I've since seen many different versions in the work of other great thinkers and teachers in the personal development movement around the globe. But it was only when I married this information with my extensive understanding of the psychology behind the human energy system that things really started to turn around dramatically in my own life. This inspired me further to evolve it in my own work so as to specifically target the issues that women face, particularly women who are coming through the divorce process. Women who need to understand the inner and outer mechanics for creating empowered new lives from scratch, and fast.

Most children grow up with dreams or distinct ideas about what they would like their lives to look like some day; what careers they would like to follow, what change they would like to make in the world, and so on.

But as little girls, particularly in the sphere of relationships, our vision for the future took on a slightly different slant from an early age. While young boys are brought up to worship power and status and taught to be tough like lions, our ideals are subtly moulded from a young age to take on a different role – to be supporters and nurturers, good little girls and sweet little lambs – the rose between the thorns. Many of us were put to bed with fairy tales of knights on white horses who would rescue us, marry us and take us off to their castles to live happily ever after. Many of us watched our parents and grandparents live out traditional roles of male as provider and female as family nurturer and homemaker. And while we came to understand, as we grew older, that these were merely stories, the deeply ingrained and powerfully manipulative expectations of the roles males and females should play in relationships, remained. Although unspoken, this continues on to this day, keeping us hooked into the romantic, but co-dependent ideal of the "knight-in-shining-armour-rescues-damsel-in-distress" lifestyle.

Growing up under these dynamics and trying to make it all fit together as an adult, especially in the face of all the mixed messages and distorted depictions in the media of what it means to be a woman, is confusing. It's become quite challenging to figure out how to live life as an empowered woman and able creator of what really matters to you as an individual.

In the lives of younger girls today, the fairy tale myth has morphed into a modern version – the dream of living celebrity lifestyles. Ask many young western girls what they want to be when they grow up and most will still answer that they want to be either "a princess", "someone famous" or "married to someone rich".

We live in a fantasy world that indulges maximum expectation and instant gratification with minimal effort. As women, at a very deep level, we hold an unconscious belief that if we behave like "good girls" in our relationships and do everything in the way that's expected of us, then life will reward us with happiness ever after and everything will work out just fine. Unfortunately, this couldn't be further from the truth.

The truth is, whether male or female, nowhere in the education system are we being taught the practice of how to set and review life goals. Yet, in line with our natural talents and abilities, they are essential to moving us in the direction of what we are striving towards. Having awareness of this would place us in the strongest possible position of being able to create the fulfilled lives that we so desire. Additionally, we would be more capable of being able to re-direct our lives whenever we choose to or need to, especially when tragedy strikes.

Instead, we live our lives day-to-day, pretty much on auto-pilot because we believe we simply have no time to live it any other way. We are directed by outer events and only have a vague sense of what it is we truly want out of life. Many of us live quietly desperate lives, easily pushed back by events that leave us feeling more and more like invisible misfits in society. We feel like victims of circumstance instead of able creators of our futures. We resign ourselves to living life from the outside in, bullied by outer events, instead of directing our lives from the inside out. And sadly, when all is said and done, when we are in our final days, we look back with so much regret.

Reflections:

Do you remember being influenced by fairy tales or images of "happily-ever-after" as a child?

Did you grow up with sets of instructions as to how little girls should behave?

Is it possible that you may still be holding on to beliefs that are causing you to have unrealistic expectations within your relationships?

The Wheel of Life

Divorce and separation is exactly the type of unplanned traumatic event that can paralyse you and leave you feeling like a victim of circumstance. This is because your priorities are shifting so suddenly and dramatically at the moment. What many of us don't fully understand is that there are eight major areas in which we all operate and make decisions in daily, whether we are conscious of it or not. At a time like this, all eight areas are tossed into the air and when they finally fall back into place their order has been completely re-arranged.

One of the most fundamental things to do at a time like this is take an in-depth look and understand each of these areas so that you can identify where the biggest change is occurring. This will help you reclaim and direct your life with purpose, and is absolutely essential to an empowered outcome.

The eight areas that make up the Wheel of Life

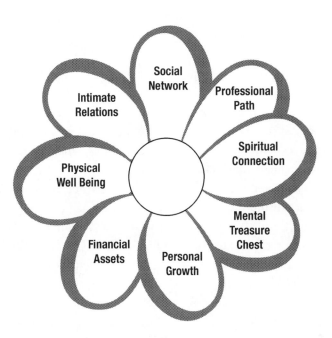

The tricky thing is that each of us usually enjoys engaging in only *some* of these areas, in line with our personal interests and abilities. But we don't enjoy the rest.

And while it's normal for most of us to invest our energy and attention more into some areas than others, what is really important is to hold a degree of ownership in every single area, particularly as a woman. Why? Because any area that you delegate entirely to someone else (spouse, friend, family member), creates a personal weak spot that leaves you potentially vulnerable.

Sharing duties and responsibilities works well, both in personal and business partnerships, where we need to work as a team but in terms of personal empowerment, it does not. And the journey of life, with all its good and bad experiences and it's ups and downs, is designed to ensure exactly that – that you expand and master every single area of your life at some point throughout your lifetime.

As women this can become particularly challenging at times. We finish our education and some of us go on to obtain university degrees. Some of us step onto the corporate ladder with great vision. Then we meet the love of our lives, get married and are soon faced with conflicting choices about whether to continue our careers or have children, and which to put first. Once we have had our children, our maternal instinct to give them the best start in life kicks in and with that choice comes the accompanying delegation of the financial areas of our lives to our partners, who reciprocate and hand over the reigns of family life.

This is a healthy and necessary exchange that works well for many couples raising children. And, naturally, we do face times in our lives when it is also necessary to make these kinds of sacrifices for others, for example looking after a spouse or family member who has taken ill. But raising a family requires the participation of both parties. Having the on-going ability to bring in an income, whether it's through a career path or a hobby, is essential for both parties. Having personal needs met is important for both parties and living a fulfilled and meaningful life, in which you have opportunities to expand as a human being and maintain your individuality and self- worth, is vital for both parties. Each party needs to be responsible enough to recognise, communicate and fairly negotiate their expectations responsibly and ethically. Otherwise it's too easy to slip into comfortable roles or unhealthy habits that can cause either party to abdicate important responsibilities, thereby creating unhealthy dependencies.

We live in a world today that's very different from generations gone by. Divorce rates have reached endemic proportions globally. In our pursuit of female liberation, the introduction of credit spending and the struggles resulting from unstable and fluctuating economies, the roles and responsibilities of women in the family have changed massively as families rely now, more than ever, on dual income. But families are being torn apart daily and many women are left with sole responsibility for raising their children, some of them on very little income and with bleak career prospects. It's time for women to re-think how we engage life with all its complexities in an ever-changing world. To establish new ground as we begin to understand how we can maintain our identity in all areas of our lives and under all circumstances - especially within the family unit.

The game of trauma and loss, which is massively driven by the level of personal power we hold in each area, is so closely linked to the heartache we experience during a breakup, that we can't even see it. Without personal weak spots, whether internal or external, real loss simply cannot exist. The Wheel of Life is a powerful tool and I've yet to find anyone who has gone through this part of my process and come out the other end with less than half of their heartache completely dissolved. It never ceases to amaze me.

Reflections:

Looking at the Wheel of Life diagram, can you begin to identify areas in which you feel confident and in control? In which areas do you feel out of control?

Making the Wheel of Life your own

When you read through this section you will clearly begin to understand why Essential Self-Care was introduced as a foundation to this process as so many of the steps are designed to empower you in each of these areas.

Let's expand each life area in the wheel, one by one, for you to gain a deeper understanding of what this looks like and how to apply it to your own life.

As you read through this section, be sure to note down any thoughts or insights that come to you, in your journal. This will be a great point of reference later on when we work with your own personal wheel of life.

1. Your Physical Well-Being

This area concerns the way in which you relate to yourself and your environment physically. It includes your overall health and vitality as well as diet and lifestyle choices. It's also concerned with how you feel about your appearance in terms of your body weight, image and personal style. How confidently you carry yourself and present yourself to the world physically.

Your physical well-being also extends to your physical environment, which includes the space in your home, your car, your office and the way in which your material possessions are ordered and accessed. Is your environment and the space that you occupy organized or cluttered?

What it looks like when you're losing power in this area:

❀ You constantly feel tired, like you're running on low energy, usually due to lack of optimal nutrition, water intake, exercise or sleep.

❀ You feel unattractive, old or frumpy and it's a struggle to find enough time in the day to spend on your own appearance.

❀ You're unable to love and accept yourself and your body as it is and every time you look in the mirror you are more focused on your perceived flaws than what's beautiful about you. You constantly compare yourself to the airbrushed images of women depicted in the media and berate yourself or criticize parts of your body for not looking the same way.

❀ Your environment (home, office, car) is cluttered, disorganised and untidy and you get that sinking feeling of overwhelm every time you look at it.

❀ You have all sorts of goals you would like to achieve or hobbies you would like to start but you feel you don't have enough energy to give to them.

Reflections:

Where, in the list above, do you recognize yourself as losing power?

Do you feel proud of who you are in this area as a woman or do you aspire to making improvements?

Can you love and accept yourself exactly as you are?

2. Your Mental Treasure Chest

This area is concerned with how you relate to others through your thought processes and how you express accumulated knowledge. The knowledge you acquire and the way in which you share it with the world is one of the most valuable assets you have. The old saying "knowledge is power" certainly is true.

In the workplace, knowledge and expertise are exchanged for higher wages, recognition and career progression. In social circles it holds influence with others and magnetizes people, connections and opportunities towards you. In relationships it breeds respect, a sense of empowerment and interesting intellectual exchanges. It also attracts exciting new opportunities.

On a much deeper level, this area is also intricately connected to how you perceive life. Do you look for the negatives instead of the positives or can you see both sides? Do you actively focus on strengths or only on weaknesses? Do you have an open or closed approach to life? Can you see change as a good thing or does your need to be in control close you off to new opportunities? The way in which you use your mind powerfully affects your choices and the way in which you continually shape the direction of your life.

Most women begin their lives in a strong place in this area. They get educated, have their own interests, build healthy social circles and begin climbing the corporate ladder. However, once they turn their full attention to family, their growth in this area often becomes a little stunted. Many stop learning new things outside of family life. As the children get older, they become more and more disconnected to the interests that once reflected their individuality and they become more and more dissatisfied with the very small political world they find themselves en-meshed in with other parents, politics at school, extended family dynamics and social circles that have a tendency to be predominantly family orientated. When divorce strikes, or when the children come of age and leave home, this inevitably results in a loss of identity in this area.

What it looks like when you're losing power in this area:

- Feeling intellectually inadequate or feeling small, like you're not participating fully with events or the world at large.

- Feeling like you're wrapped up in a very limited reality, constantly dealing with mundane and routine issues.

- Not earning enough money in exchange for your skills and abilities.

- A negative attitude towards what you can achieve in the future and a feeling of being powerless to change it.

❀ Lacking the confidence to socialise in certain circles or feeling like a social wallflower because you are unable to contribute to intellectually orientated conversations.

❀ Criticizing anyone you perceive as intellectually threatening in an attempt to feel better about yourself.

❀ Feeling that nobody hears or sees you and that your opinion doesn't really count.

Reflections:

Do any of the above situations resonate in any way with you?

When and where did you withdraw from accumulating knowledge in your life? Isn't it good to know that this can easily be remedied?

3. Your Spiritual Connection

This area is concerned with your connection to your intuitive self and your intimate relationship with a higher power, whether you prefer to reference this as God, Higher Self, Universe, etc.

Here we find another powerful area that yields high returns on investment. In a later chapter on self esteem I speak extensively about the role that inner connectedness plays in your ability to handle everything that comes your way in life and the ability to follow your inner voice, something that I believe is an essential ingredient for success in life.

Your spiritual connection is not to be confused with your personal development. Yet, when the two are successfully combined, something truly beautiful emerges. Your spiritual connection is about knowing who you are at a higher level. It's about your ability to connect to your own intuitive guidance, have faith in a force greater than yourself that guides your life and be able to follow this faithfully. It's not linked to any particular religion or organisation. It's a highly personal relationship and experience that empowers you. It's an "inner" connectedness to wisdom and a knowing that allows you to navigate the choices you face. It's totally exclusive of any outer influence from people and events.

Personal development on the other hand, is the acquisition of knowledge that allows you to refine aspects of your personality so that you can better perceive and overcome the challenges of everyday life and expand a greater vision for the things you would like to create and attain in life. It is "outer based", connected to learning and intimately linked to interaction and influence from the world around you.

Many people mistakenly believe that their personal development is actually their spiritual practice and this kind of thinking will get you into real trouble because you'll start living life reactively from the outside in, instead of creating from the inside out.

Most people feel very disconnected as they stumble through their daily lives. They are anxious, they worry excessively about things that are beyond their control, they are afraid and so they run from one quick fix to another. Who can blame them? In many ways life is constantly changing and uncertainty and insecurity have become part of the structure of daily life in our society. Never has it been more important to be able to quiet your thoughts, find stillness in whatever way works best for you and connect within to your own guidance. Meditation, yoga, tai chi and deep breathing are all excellent ways of doing this and they are becoming more and more popular.

You have a very distinct path to walk in life and it is yours. You were born with a guidance system that is designed to give you constant feedback so you can always find your way. That guidance system is e-motion (energy in motion) and when you feel bad, your guidance is feeding back to you that something is not working and needs to be changed (either on the inside, or the outside). The worst thing you can do when you hear that is run off to well meaning family and friends, psychics or even personal development courses and tap THEIR guidance systems as a point of reference for finding your own solution. Why? Because they can only be reference points for their own belief systems and philosophies and they will always advise you according to that. Engaging in this type of behaviour over a long period of time will leave you feeling disconnected and will ultimately result in the development of a deep distrust in your own decisions, encouraging you to blame others when things go wrong.

This area grows healthy when you are able to take on board advice from others, while ultimately following your own truth. This area also grows healthy when you begin to have faith in a power greater than yourself that guides your life through the channel of your own intuition. Anxiety and despair dissolve and resistance is released when you are able to recognise that your life is always meaningfully directed. Then you can connect the dots and feel confident enough to trust and follow the signs.

What it looks like when you're losing power in this area:

❀ You don't like your own company and need to be around others so you can drown out your own reality in exchange for theirs.

❀ You don't trust your own knowing and constantly seek external validation that you are on the right track.

❀ You distrust your own truth and, as a result, find it difficult to make decisions on your own.

❀ You are too wrapped up in the lives and decisions of others.

❀ You are easily influenced by the opinions of others and that influence often causes you to make unhealthy decisions for your life. When things go wrong you blame those whose opinions you took on board.

✿ You have goals for your life but you are often swayed off track by the opinions of friends, family or colleagues.

Reflections:

Can you relate to any of the above ways in which you may have lost connection to yourself?

Can you give yourself permission to trust yourself to make the right decisions for what you need in life right now?

4. Your Professional Path

This area is concerned with the service that you offer to the world, often in exchange for money, and is connected to your sense of purpose. When humans beings are not contributing to their families, communities or society, in one way or another, they start to feel worthless and depressed.

Ironically, many people think of this area as the boring chore they have to get up and participate in everyday just to make enough money to get by. They fail to recognise that even by being a small part of any organisation, the skills and influence they bring to that organization play a vital role in the delivery of that service to the world. Equally, they are an integral part of the economy and the opportunities that their organisation generates globally through its services. A cleaner at Nasa was once asked, as he was sweeping the floor, if he enjoyed keeping the floors of Nasa clean. He replied "I don't clean the floors of Nasa, I send people into space". He got it. He got that he was a vital cog in the machine called Nasa.

Too many teenage girls chase the fantasy of Hollywood house-wives without any real understanding of the downsides that come along with living that type of lifestyle. It's easy and often sad to predict where, without intervention, the lives of these young girls are headed because they are not pursuing empowerment in this area.

Your professional path often goes hand-in-hand with your Mental Treasure Chest. I believe it's really important that we continually grow and stretch ourselves. Even if you have chosen to give up your career to be home with your children, one of the greatest contributions you can make to the world, I still believe that it's healthy to keep a connection to your professional path. Even if you maintain aspects of it on a part-time basis as a hobby until you decide to take it up full time again. Doing this keeps you connected to your own sense of self and allows you to be able to convert your inner resources back into monetary exchange again when you feel ready to do so.

The pressure that many divorced women face today, particularly if they have been supported financially by their husbands for extended periods of time, is the shocking reality that, not only do they have to deal with the emotional challenges of the divorce, but they will also have to go back out into the workplace in a world that has changed drastically in the time they have been away from it. This can be a terrifying predicament to find yourself in and, if you continue to allow fear to paralyse you and refuse to reclaim your power in this area, it can seriously impact your entire future.

The less connected you are to contributing to life as a whole, the more the walls of your life will close in. Eventually you will start to feel insecure and worthless, like you're stuck in a limited world that's weighing you down and leaving you feeling very small indeed.

What it looks like when you're losing power in this area:

❀ You feel a loss of connection to your purpose, particularly when your children are grown up and have left home.

❀ You form new intimate relationships from a place of dependency because you are afraid to take ownership of your own professional path.

❀ You feel insecure, intimidated and inadequate in the company of powerful women with successful careers.

❀ Your dependency on financial support drives you to become controlling and manipulative in relationships and you often find yourself putting down other women comparatively to feel better about yourself.

Reflections:

Have you allowed your professional path to slide? Will you need to return to work after your divorce?

If so, which industries or companies inspire you and make you feel you would like to be a part of what they are contributing to the world?

If not, what hobby or activity can you begin that reflects your unique individual nature and contributes to your family or community in a way that fulfills you?

5. Your Financial Assets

This area is concerned with the amount of savings and investments you have set aside to provide for your future and the way in which you can grow your existing assets so that, in the longer term, your money works for you instead of you working for your money.

What needs to be emphasized here is that this area is not about acquiring financial assets from which to consistently draw on to buy the things you want in life. It's about building long-term financial assets that provide greater security and freedom for your future. In our world of "fantastic plastic" and "instant gratification" most of us have lost sight of the true value of money and given way to living on credit, never actually earning and saving our money before spending it. This has been one of the biggest lessons of all the great recessions of our time, yet we never seem to create this discipline in our culture.

I believe we should be taught, through our education systems if not by our parents, how to save and invest our income wisely. A good rule of thumb is to consistently aim to put away 10% of your earnings each month and increase this amount at least twice a year.

When I learnt the formula for working out the cost of living into my retirement age, taking the rate of inflation into account, I actually had a couple of sleepless nights! Yet this is something that many of us never think about and, in our failure to plan, we are planning to fail as future elderly citizens. If you're roughly middle aged and you're hoping to retire on state pensions, please trust me when I tell you that this won't nearly be enough once you actually reach retirement age - and that's if it's even available as an option anymore.

Coming through divorce and separation can be a big wake up call in the area of finance. It causes the most legal conflict as both parties battle it out to secure as much for their future as possible. It's the cause of so much bitterness and resentment and it's often shocking when you watch the person you loved for so long, in many cases the father of your children, suddenly turn on the family and do his best to find a way of leaving you with as little money as he is legally bound to.

When I separated from my husband I would never have dreamed that things could get quite as nasty as they did. Thankfully, in our case, it was short lived but, if you find yourself in this situation, it's important to know that you do have legal rights and that the law protects women now, more than ever, so make sure you seek legal advice from a good solicitor (this was covered in the earlier chapter on Essential Self-Care).

The important thing to remember if you feel powerless in this area is that you will need to map out a plan for getting yourself into a position where you can begin to save. I once saw a story on Oprah about a woman who earned $1,200 per month working in an office admin role. She lived alone. Other than a small inheritance of $400 left to her by her father when he died, she had no additional income other than a monthly salary of $1200 and the only way she could save was to put away a dollar a day and then, slowly, be savvy about investing her money as it grew. She did this throughout her life and eventually as her humble bank balance grew, so did some of the opportunities that came her way (yes, money is energy and if you look after it and respect it, it attracts more money). By the time she reached retirement she had saved a million dollars, just by tending this area everyday throughout her life.

Pay attention to your relationship with money. Are you comfortable with it? The way you handle money, the things you choose to invest it in and the beliefs you have around it have a massive impact on how much of it flows into or out of your life. If you respect it, it will work for you and you will be its master. If you don't, it will work against you and you will be its slave.

What it looks like when you're losing power in this area:

🌸 You feel uncomfortable about the idea of handling, receiving or parting with money or you could have a strong attachment to feelings of monetary lack.

🌸 You feel dependent on others to handle money on your behalf or provide financially for your survival or you may have an entitlement mentality (the world owes me) instead of an empowered mentality (I am capable of providing for myself and my future).

❀ Your general lack of financial discipline negatively impacts your self-esteem and you find yourself spending excessively in an attempt to feel better about yourself.

❀ You don't know how to save. You have no control over your income and outgoings.

❀ You choose not to pay bills or handle financial matters successfully in your relationships. This causes you to lose your grip on the true value of money.

❀ You have credit card, store card and loan debts and you have no idea how you are going to pay them off.

❀ You were raised with negative beliefs about how hard it is to earn money and you have negative beliefs about money being the root of all evil and wealthy people being greedy, therefore you believe it's bad to have money in your life.

Reflections:

What limiting beliefs and behaviours do you engage around money?

Do you believe that you are capable of making more than enough to provide for yourself now and into the future?

Do you save regularly? If not, when will you start?

What interests, hobbies, knowledge and personal traits do you possess that would be worth a fortune if you were to harness them to generate cash?

6. Your Intimate Relationships

This area is concerned with your relationships with those closest to you - your birth family, your life partner and your children.

This area offers the greatest growth potential to the human soul of all the areas because it pushes our buttons. It is only through living and engaging in the rich contrast that our closest relationships provide, that we grow throughout life.

As difficult as some of our closest relationships can sometimes be, especially if we have made the choice to cut out members of our birth family for whatever reason, we must begin to understand that it is the nature of those relationships that have shaped the best of who we are today. We must always take a broader view, find the perfection and make peace within our hearts.

I travelled away from my home country and my family at a fairly young age and started a new life in a different country when I got married. But I was always amazed at how quickly "family members" emerged on my travels. By this I mean that people would show up and take on a motherly role, a fatherly role and a brotherly role in my life. Even new friends that I made seemed to carry the characteristics of friends back home. No matter which new location I moved to, this pattern would continually repeat. Not that I lost touch with my own family at all – I spoke with them every week and still do and I visit them every year - it's just that life abhors a vacuum and if we really look, anything that we see as "missing" from our lives, is always close by, waiting for recognition and acceptance.

When this area of your life is strong, you have healthy intimate relationships and you are able to recognize surrogate friends and family whenever you are away from your own. You are also able to find the deeper truths to challenges you have experienced within your birth family, your intimate relationships and the new family you may have created. You are able to let go of grudges because this understanding brings great love and peace and you value the gifts gained from each interaction, even those that you once labelled as unforgiveable.

What it looks like when you're losing power in this area:

❀ You carry deep unhealed wounds from past relationships, which affect your new relationships.

❀ You distrust new relationships that come into your life as you attempt to "protect" yourself from others.

❀ You fail to acknowledge, communicate or appreciate the good in your family or your partner, which ultimately leads to a breakdown in the relationship.

❀ You feel misunderstood and alone at a deep level, even when others are around you.

❀ You think others are constantly attacking you and you feel afraid to express your true opinions and ideas at times.

Reflections:

Who are your most beloved nearest and dearest?

When last did you let them know how much you love and appreciate them?

What small thing can you do today to brighten up a loved one's life by showing your care and appreciation for them?

7. Your Social Network

This area is concerned with the circle of friends that you interact with and also the influence you have within that circle.

When we are single this area of our lives often expands as we go out, meet new people and expose ourselves to new activities. But often, once we are get into a new relationship, we make the mistake of not tending our gardens of friendship very well and, as life takes over and we focus most of our attention on our partners and our families, good friends sometimes fall by the wayside.

As we move through life growing and changing as individuals in relation to our changing circumstances, the people we are friends with naturally change to reflect this and that's normal. If you have friends that you have known from childhood and you are able to keep a healthy friendship for life, that's something very special and to be cherished. If you find yourself travelling and moving around a lot as I did in my marriage (and as many women do these days), you can easily begin to feel isolated and depend too heavily on your partner for the different types of company that a variety of people would provide. This can put a lot of strain on the relationship if it continues long term.

Although it may sound a little obvious, this is an area that I cannot encourage enough that you take the time and energy to keep strong. Spending enough time building and maintaining quality relationships is the aim here, even if you have to schedule in regular time for socials.

Coming through divorce and separation is one of the times when you will truly draw great strength and comfort from your real friends. You can balance time spent healing with time spent socialising, providing some light-hearted fun when needed. This builds new social circles and introduces you to all sorts of new people that can help you to positively re-shape your life.

It's been proven that a healthy social network has a massive impact on self-esteem as well as the immune system. The human body depends massively on an intricate design of healthy internal networks to maintain optimum function and the human psyche is no different. While some of us prefer to network within a wide framework and have many acquaintances, others prefer a smaller, more intimate circle. Both are fine but having them and keeping them is the key.

What it looks like when you're losing power in this area:

🌸 You feel isolated, cut off and alone.

🌸 You lack the necessary opportunities and connections when you need assistance.

🌸 You don't make friends easily and you have a natural tendency to distrust others.

🌸 You feel that others are out to get you, therefore you don't trust them.

🌸 You feel afraid and you prefer to carry the burden of life on your shoulders alone, while secretly wishing it wasn't so.

🌸 You can't open up to others for fear of being judged or you feel you aren't fun to be with and feel inadequate.

Reflections:

How healthy is your social network? Do you share quality relationships within your networks?

Are you able to open up and be yourself?

Think of one new thing you can do today to increase the amount of people you are exposed to.

8. Your Personal Growth

More and more this is becoming an essential part of societal progression. This area is concerned with your growth and development as it relates to learning and practising mastery over your thoughts and emotions as well as expanding your interpersonal skills and influence within your familial, social and professional circles. In a way, it's almost a healthy rolling together of all the other areas integrated with the practice of solid self-esteem and personal boundaries (still to come in later chapters).

I used to think that this area was simply a part of the Mental Treasure Chest area and that it was just another form of learning that was preferable to some people. But then I started to notice how many people who came from very impressive academic backgrounds, held positions of power and enjoyed exceptional wealth, still lived empty and selfish lives, alienating the people around them. They had a wealth of knowledge and a healthy bank balance to show for it, but behaved in a rude, arrogant and self-righteous manner. And, because they didn't care how many people they needed to walk over to get what they wanted, it was easy to see that their ultimate success had a glass ceiling as so much of what they did to others often led to their own demise.

When I returned to work in London as part of the process of building my own life back, I worked for a boutique style company in which the owners were both extremely successful and wealthy. Their interpersonal skills, however, were totally lacking. They behaved in a highly arrogant manner towards members of staff, suppliers and even potential customers. They treated their staff as inferior, barely greeting them, and refused to invest in equipping them with the resources required for being able to do the job properly and grow to their full potential. There was so much talent there, so much potential for the company to explode on the global market but it was so obvious to see that, because of poor communication and poor internal relations, staff turnover occurred at a ferocious rate. With such a weak internal network, how on earth could their external network grow to reflect anything beyond that?

The world in which success is obtained solely through individual effort, no longer exists. It has ended. With the advent of social media, and the transparency it has introduced into our culture, we now live in a world where collaboration is the only true path to success. The invention of social media platforms may still be fairly new in terms of personal and professional users but there is no denying that it's the way forward. Anyone who thinks that they don't need to invest in their own growth or the growth of their relationships with others is on a road with a dead end.

Never has it been more important for us to equip ourselves with tools for honouring ourselves and one another and to know how to balance the two without causing damage.

There are hundreds of good personal development books out there by authors like Anthony Robbins, Sandra Anne Taylor, Louise Hay, Steven Covey and many more. I recommend you also look into some good personal development seminars at which you are guaranteed to meet some really lovely, like-minded people. This is an area so worth exploring and developing and my number one piece of advice to you is this: much like this book that you are reading, don't just learn the information – put it into practice! Otherwise you're at risk of becoming a personal development junkie. You'll go from one seminar to the next to get your fix but never integrate the information enough to make the necessary changes that will so greatly enhance your life.

What it looks like when you're losing power in this area:

- You feel like a victim, you can't comprehend that things aren't happening to you but through you.

- You give up personal interests and hobbies that usually bring you joy in order to please others.

- You blame others for things that go wrong in your life, you feel angry and afraid.

- You can be overly critical and judgmental of those around you.

- You don't take responsibility for the changes you want to make in your life and you get your energy by taking it from others.

❁ You are not self-aware and therefore you try to control others.

❁ You don't understand why life doesn't work for you.

Reflections:

How do you feel about the concept of personal growth?

Are you willing to take full responsibility for your life and release the need to blame others altogether?

Do you like the idea of collaborating with others? Would you be willing to do what it takes to learn to trust yourself and develop personal and professional relations with others?

Creating a new vision for your life

Now that we've explored the many facets contained within the Wheel of Life and had some insights as to where you are empowered and where you are losing power, let's move on to the next crucial stage of building a new vision for each area.

Healing Action Step

Using the wheel to create your vision of empowerment

In your notebook, and using the chart below as a guide, write down each area contained within the Wheel of Life.

Now, for each of these areas, write down what you would ultimately love to achieve or create in that area. You need only write two or three short sentences here.

Life area	What I Would Love This Area to Look Like...
Physical Well-Being	
Mental Treasure Chest	
Spiritual Connection	
Professional Path	
Financial Assets	
Intimate Relationships	
Social Network	
Personal Growth	

It's key to remember, as you complete this exercise, that you need to keep it real, achievable and in line with the person you are and the things that are important to you. Remember also that you are the one who is ultimately going to bring about the changes you are writing down. If you're financially down and out and you write in the area of "Financial Assets" that you want millions of pounds or dollars in the bank, then you will need to be able to come up with an action plan for authentically achieving that **without someone else providing the money for you.** Otherwise you'll just be right back to square one, starting a new cycle of disempowerment all over again.

If you feel you don't have enough friends and you write in the area of "Social Network" that you would love to have twenty-five good friends, great! But know that you will be the one responsible for getting that result so, while I really do encourage you to *stretch* yourself in this exercise, please ensure that your goals are attainable in the short to medium term.

Once you've achieved your goals you can re-do this exercise and stretch out the boundaries some more. As a matter of fact I encourage you to do this exercise at least twice a year if you want to continue investing progressively into your future.

Auditing your Wheel of Life

Once you have completed your list of what you would love each area of your Wheel of Life to look like in the future, its time for the final step – working out what your levels of empowerment currently are in these areas.

Healing Action Step

Find your empowerment strengths and challenges

Sit quietly and look at each area. Ask yourself honestly, how empowered you are AT THIS MOMENT in relation to what you wrote down. Score it as a percentage. For example, if you said under "Physical Well-Being" that you would love to have a certain image or style or enjoy a healthy diet that leads to achieving a particular weight and you're already almost there, then you will score yourself at around 80% to 90% empowered in that area. If you would love to enjoy a wide social circle but you don't like socialising and have only one or two friends, you may want to score yourself around 20% empowered in that area.

This is an intuitive exercise so you need to trust yourself and the answers that come up for you.

Complete the exercise and then take all the areas and percentage scores you wrote down - ordering them from highest to lowest. If you scored two or three areas with exactly the same percentage, ask yourself "If I could only take one of these forward into my future, which would it be?" You will find that one of them will have a slightly higher priority so put that one before the other.

For example:

Physical Well-Being	90%
Spiritual Connection	70%
Professional Path	65%
Mental Treasure Chest	45%
Intimate Relationships	45%
Social Network	40%
Personal Growth	30%
Financial Assets	25%

Once you have completed your list, take a look at the three areas at the *bottom* of the list (those with the lowest scores). Right there you will find the areas of your life in which you are currently the most disempowered and that are bringing up the most fear for you. These are the areas that are being flagged up for growth and evolution through your divorce orseparation. **These are your key areas of focus for empowerment as you move forward to building a whole and self-fulfilled life.**

I urge you at this point to take 100% responsibility and commit wholeheartedly to making the changes necessary to improve these bottom three areas. I know this may seem scary at the moment, particularly if you're looking at "Professional Path", "Financial Assets" and "Social Network" because this means you are really not getting a whole lot of support right now. But please trust me on this – herein lies your biggest challenge but also your greatest opportunity to take back REAL power in your life. Face your fears head on. You will amaze yourself at the person you will become and you CAN do it. I know because I did it, against all the odds. We will deal with the fear in a later chapter but for now, you're discovering more about who you are.

As I've said before, time will not heal your wounds - time only numbs the unresolved emotions and distorted conclusions that remain at the end of the relationship. By taking responsibility for your part in events and knowing who you are and where you are headed next, you can induce real healing and increase your self-confidence.

Connect the dots

Look back at the answers you wrote in your journal in the previous chapter where you gave the reasons for how your life will benefit now that you are free of the relationship.

✿ Can you see how much of what you identified there ties in with your Wheel of Life audit?

❁ Can you see how being in the relationship was holding you back or holding you in a disempowered place in certain areas? Yes it's been comfortable but it's time for change.

❁ Can you begin to identify a way forward in terms of which key areas you need to develop that are unique to yourself?

It's time for evolution. You are a powerfully creative being, whether you are aware of it or not. It's time to direct your energy and resources into building a beautiful new life. This is the profound second chance you have been given to live a life that you love.

Now, let's get you off that emotional rollercoaster!

Chapter 4

Balancing your Mind and Emotions

"Nobody can really hurt you. They're only giving you their observation and you are giving it meaning. But you get to decide what that meaning is."

— Desiree Marie Leedo —

If you are applying all the Essential Self-Care tools effectively, you are most likely already feeling calmer, emotionally. You may still have your rollercoaster days or flip between sadness, anger, helplessness and upset, but on the whole you should be feeling a lot more in control and better able to deal with what's going on around you. Completing your wheel of life has also given you greater clarity and insight into the new direction your life is taking and, as you work with your mind and emotions throughout this chapter, your wheel of life will gain further strength and meaning.

We are now deepening the psychological work as I help you

achieve a more balanced perspective and, consequently, a more balanced emotional state by equipping you with some basic tools to apply to your own life. At the moment you're still on a bit of a see-saw. One day you feel outraged and look down at your ex as inferior and the next day you feel inferior yourself because you're out of control and fearful of the future.

While there is a natural psychology to the process of breaking up that consists of seven distinct stages, one of the things that many people do is bounce between stages or remain stuck in one stage for far too long, sometimes even decades. Meaning and true acceptance only come by moving through each and every one of these seven stages.

The Seven Psychological Stages of Divorce

As I moved through my own divorce experience and spoke with many other women who did the same, I distinctly noticed seven stages through which we all must pass to complete the healing process. Furthermore, it became evident that we can move through these stages in a matter of weeks, months, years or even decades, depending on whether or not we have a healthy construct in place for moving us through the process!

My deepest desire is that, by working through this book, you get there in a matter of weeks and months instead of years and decades.

As you read through the following stages, see if you can identify where you are right now:

1. Shock

Your first reaction will predominantly be shock, especially if it's sudden. This state is void of emotion and evokes a type of numb disbelief. You feel out of sorts, as if you're watching events from outside your own body and you're prone to staring off into space and losing time. Restful sleep evades you as your mind struggles to adjust to what is happening.

2. Denial

Shock subsides and reality kicks in. This is the phase during which you repeatedly contact your partner, attempting to have conversations that verify that it really is over. Doubt creeps in and you look for ways to salvage the relationship. You want to negotiate and you are willing to sacrifice your truth and yourself in a last ditch attempt to hold the crumbling relationship together.

3. Anger and Resentment

Once there is no question that it's over, anger kicks in. This can be in a variety of forms – from the "flashing raw" anger to the more subtle "mental justification" anger. During this stage you flip between fixating on the good things about the relationship and the rage of betrayal for all the 'false promises' made in your wedding vows. You'll count every sacrifice you ever made in the face of your rejection and you'll make new vows to yourself never to trust again. This is an intense phase and it's important to move out of this phase fairly quickly as it can be very damaging, particularly if fuelled by malicious and destructive feelings of revenge.

4. Fear and Depression

As the reality of all the immediate to long-term change you face sets in, you start looking ahead from a distorted perspective. Any area of your life in which you now feel out of control or disempowered (ie. career, finance, etc.) will surface as an issue, while feelings of being a failure and facing a future filled with loss and uncertainty leave you spiralling into a state of depression. You start battling with a myriad of "what-if's" as you bounce back and forth between fear and helplessness, validating your feelings of resignation and depression.

5. Meaning and Purpose

Now you slowly begin to formulate your thoughts and emotions into questions from which you seek meaning and purpose behind the breakup. Here you must take responsibility for your part in the event and find the deeper meaning – the lesson or the gift - before you can move on.

What you're really going through here is a type of identity crisis in which you understand at a very deep level that change is demanded of you. What you really start asking is "Why has this happened, who am I now and how do I move forward?"

This is the death and re-birth stage during which some people seek professional help. It is a critical stage to overcome because, if left unprocessed, you may not move past this stage and continue to bounce back and forth between this stage and the third stage (between "anger, resentment, fear, and depression) for as long as it takes!

Many people spend decades stuck here and never heal completely. Some shut down emotionally and close themselves off for fear of being hurt again while others carry their distorted perceptions around as baggage from one failed relationship to the next.

6. Acceptance and Closure

When your thoughts and emotions have been properly ordered and your questions sufficiently answered for you to connect with the meaning and purpose behind the event, you reach the stage of acceptance and closure. A deeper wisdom results and you are now able to view the situation and your life from a broader perspective with a clearer understanding of who you are now and where your life is next headed.

7. Love and Gratitude

This is the final stage of the process and it is often rare for people to attain by themselves. From this place you are able to look back on your relationship with a heart full of love and absolute appreciation. Here you reach a level of true gratitude for the gift and opportunity that your ex has given you. It's a place of higher understanding from which you can move forward with absolute inner peace and grace, regardless of how your ex is reacting. You are free.

The purpose of my entire process, as laid out step-by-step in each chapter of this book, is to move you through these seven stages fast.

However, having said that, this is a difficult chapter for me to write as this part of the process is never a "one-size-fits-all" solution. Each person who walks through my door for consultation brings with them a different cocktail of emotions that need to be healed and I am only too aware that I am unable to work individually with you and your specific circumstances in person via the medium of this book.

The gift in the grief

The first thing to remember when you are separating from a long-term relationship is that you are not alone! There are literally thousands of women around the world, some in far more dire situations, going through this same experience as well.

There is nothing wrong with you. You haven't failed. You're not unworthy. You're just someone going through an event called divorce because there is a life ahead of you that holds more potential than the one you are currently living - whether it feels that way right now, or not. And you'll get through this. You will thrive and be happy again and someday in the future, you will even be grateful that all this happened.

Every challenging and traumatic event that life brings holds the exact equal degree of blessings that become evident over a period of time - something I like to call "the gift in the grief". The more challenge you face, the greater the gift that emerges as time goes by.

Fiona's Story...

One of my clients, Fiona, was in her mid-thirties when her husband left her. Naturally, she was devastated. She tried everything to work it out and begged him to attend counselling with her, but he refused. She had spent a few years trying to get over him before she finally came to see me. Not long after our sessions ended, when she was finally back on track with her life, she found out that he had gone on to marry the woman he had been having an affair with while they were married. He had since also developed a serious and incurable illness. While she was extremely sympathetic and did everything she could to offer her support, she also realized that, had she still been with him, her newly established and thriving international business would never have got off the ground.

There are two ways to reach gratitude when challenging events occur in our lives.

❀ Allow years and even decades to go by, jumping from one relationship to the next while learning to love and trust again - until life eventually proves, over time, that what happened was the best thing for you.

❀ Take responsibility for your part in events, take ownership of your healing and ask the kind of questions that help you recognise the gifts and new direction that is emerging. Then decide, from a place of real inner connectedness, what type of limitless future you want to create, get out there and make it happen.

Too many women opt for the first option, fumbling around in the depths of their emotions in an attempt to find peace and move on. When I was going through my darkest days, I often wished that I had someone or something to guide me through my feelings of anger and betrayal - to really show me how to build a self-fulfilled new life, from the ground up. But now I am grateful that I was forced to find my own way. Because this is the gift in my grief – that I am able to reach out to women all over the world, offering them a different choice and making a difference to their lives.

Yes, you're going through a tough time, but remember you are so much more than all of this. There is a part of you that knows exactly why you are here and where you are headed next. It knows the greater plan, the many gifts and opportunities coming your way and it loves you enough to guide you patiently and lovingly to that place. Are you willing to let go and trust this part of yourself? Are you willing to be still and listen? Can you surrender your fears and rest in the stillness? Herein lies true peace of mind.

Understanding the mechanics of emotion

When it comes to balancing emotions and getting off that self-destructive rollercoaster, it's helpful to understand the exchange between your mind and emotions. This occurs so rapidly and unconsciously that you are usually oblivious to how one impacts the other. Gaining insight into this sequence of events can, however, go a long way in helping you to make changes.

⁂ First, you have a **perception** of what is occurring:
For example, you notice that the space around you seems empty. He's gone, the phone is quiet and there's just a big hole left in the life that you shared.

❁ Then you think a **thought**, based on that perception:
You wonder where it all started to go wrong. Why he really left and what you did to cause it. You wonder if you will always be alone or if you'll ever meet someone else.

❁ This immediately produces a corresponding **emotion**:
You feel lonely, rejected and unlovable. You begin to feel sad and start to cry about what's happening.

❁ That emotion sparks off a **chemical reaction** in your body:
The emotion sends a message to your brain about what's happening and how the body should prepare itself in response. Every cell hears the call and the internal mechanics are altered to compensate. When you feel angry, resentful, sad or afraid, you are literally telling your brain to prepare your body for self-rejection or attack. And trust me, every cell in your body hears the message and re-arranges its function accordingly.

Perception is everything and at a time like this I guarantee you that much of your perception is somewhat distorted. It's probably becoming obvious to you that emotions are most profoundly balanced by balancing perceptions first.

Reflections:

Can you see how easy it is to frighten yourself or hurt yourself by choosing faulty perceptions?

If you noticed the emptiness around you, would it be better to think about who has been stepping in lately with emotional support in the place of your ex?

Are you willing to choose to view things differently in the moments that make you sad?

Change your mind - change your emotions

When real balance occurs on the level of perception, emotion is instantaneously dissolved and the physical body moves back into a state of equilibrium.

Remember, you are a powerful creator and you already have your feet planted firmly on the path of creating an amazing new life, even if you can't quite feel it yet. With each small step you take you are making progress so keep going.

You are the cause of your own effect. You are your greatest healer.

A wise man once taught me that healing cannot occur and no therapy is ever complete until cause and effect are aligned within the time/space continuum. What this means is that for every cause, there is an effect. For every action, there is a reaction. But it's the separation of cause from effect by time and space that causes us to become temporarily blinded to the fact that we are both the cause and the effect of what we draw into our lives.

Mirror... Mirror...

Every person, event and circumstance that you draw into your life is there as a mirror of, and a guide for, some aspect of yourself - no matter how big or small. This forms the basis of human growth and evolution. How else would we actually be able to see ourselves if it weren't for the reflective mirror of human relationships? Sadly, because we are separated from that which exists outside of our physical bodies by space and time, when people and events that we've magnetized as reflections of our innermost selves actually show up within our experience, we're often completely oblivious to the fact that we had anything to do with their creation. Instead we point fingers at others, holding them accountable for our experiences, particularly when relationship dynamics have moved out of sync.

By understanding that healing will never occur until you close the gap between the actual event and yourself as a participative creator in that event, you will also understand that you cannot heal from your divorce until you own yourself through the mirror of your ex. Once you take full ownership of your part and see yourself as the source, the trauma dissolves and you are fully back in the driver's seat of your life.

I know that's a tall order. Up to now you have most likely felt like you'd like to rip his head off! Just relax, I'll talk you through this.

Healing Action Step

What do you see in the Mirror?

Step One: What has upset you the most?
Right now, I would like you to use your journal and make a list of all the behaviours from your ex that you still feel angry about in this moment. The list can be as long as you like, in no particular order and written exactly as it comes out of your head, no matter how random. They should include:

• Behaviours and actions from him that have upset you (e.g. he cheated, he lied, he is disrespectful, he broke his promise to me, he hurt me, he took the best years of my life, etc.)

Once your list is complete I would like you to look over it and pick out the top three behaviours or actions that have got you most upset. Write them down.

    For example:
    1. He cheated on me
    2. He lied to me
    3. He broke his promise to me

Step Two: Who's cheating who?

Now that you have your list, start a new page, putting the first item at the top of the page as a heading. Do the same for the second and third items, placing each on a separate page.

Underneath the heading, write a new heading that says: The mirror of...(insert the item on your list).

So now, your first page (which contains your first item) should look something like this:

1. *He cheated on me*
   The mirror of cheating

Now I want you to look within. I want you to fill up the rest of the page with all the ways in which you have cheated yourself through the years in your own life. It could be that you have cheated yourself out of time or cheated yourself out of personal interests or that you cheated yourself by not completing certain tasks that are important to you. I want you to really think about this and look into each area of your life, using your wheel of life if needed.

Complete this exercise for each of the three items on your list and then go through all remaining items on your original list, checking for any other major upsetting issues. When you look back now, you will probably find that some behaviours/ actions you first wrote down are slightly repetitive and seem redundant. You can delete those and continue to work only with those that still feel relevant.

Nobody rejects us until we reject ourselves. Issues of low self-esteem and self-worth are all deeply intimate forms of personal rejection. In a later chapter we will be looking at how to activate core self-esteem but, for now, just continue to work through the items on your list as effectively as you can.

Please don't fall into patterns of self-blame and self-judgement while you complete this exercise – this will only reinforce hurt. Instead, realise that your ex holds a behavioural pattern that locked into yours. It's not that he's better and that's why he took off. He cannot run away. He will only attract the next perfect match to the pattern that he holds. But for you, it's time to evolve.

Step Three: How would you like things to be?
Go back over your list from step two and under each behaviour or action, write down at least one thing you can do to change the way you are treating yourself.
For example:

1. He cheated on me
   The mirror of cheating

I cheat myself by prioritizing everyone else

Things I can do to change this behaviour:
• I'll take at least 15-30 minutes for myself at the start of each day to reflect on my needs and prioritise what is important to me.

• I'll take up that class (or other personal interest) that I've always wanted to take.

• I will set aside some quiet time to read or study each evening from now on.

• I will learn to say **No** to others sometimes.

These may seem like simple examples but you will know exactly what you need in your own life based on your own answers. I encourage you to complete this exercise in its entirety - there is much healing and self-discovery that awaits you here.

Ten steps to creating emotional balance

I know all too well how easy it is to turn on yourself at a time like this and blame yourself for everything that's happened, putting all the failure in your own camp and distorting the facts. I assure you that there's a bigger picture to life. I want to show you this as much as I possibly can in these next ten steps so that you can begin to see that the way events actually unfold versus the way you think they will unfold, are often vastly different.

At times, I'll be taking you into the future, even though, up until now, I've encouraged you to remain in the present as much as possible while you are healing. Bear with me on this – sometimes breaking from the present to consider multiple potential outcomes is enlightening and empowering and can relieve you of much unnecessary hurt.

These next ten steps (and corresponding exercises) include the most common distorted perceptions that contribute to the emotional distress of women whose partners have walked out on the relationship.

Step One: Don't devalue yourself or your life

Okay, let's face it, it's a challenging time and at some point you are definitely going to feel that you have failed. But is that really true or is that just a societal judgement that we unconsciously take on board without needing to? I don't mean to sound flippant here, or make less of the memories, life and family you built up with your partner, but the general view of divorce in our culture needs to change.

Divorce is not a condition and should not be subject to the hideous stigma that's sometimes attached to it. It's not a life sentence. It's a transformative event that leads BOTH parties to healthier, more expansive horizons, regardless of the circumstances and drama that surrounds it. Much of the fear and heartache we attach to it comes from our own resistance to change and to what we consider "acceptable" in our lives. I invite you to step out of this mindset. Hold your head up high and don't hold back. Be proud of who you are and be willing to share your experience calmly, without feeling intimidated by the opinions of others.

Many women fall into the trap of devaluing their existence when their partners walk out the door. They believe that they are unable to be who they are or live without the qualities their partners brought to the relationship. That's because they have become so identified with their partner that they have lost their connection to who they are as an individual. I've even seen women devalue themselves because of simple things, like not knowing how to pay a bill or change a lightbulb! They measure their self-worth against their inability to execute easy-to-learn, simple activities like this.

Other women measure their value against their partners' personality traits. For example, "he was always the life and soul of the party and now that he's gone, I won't socialise as much". When I hear things like this, I immediately take these women back through their relationships and look for all the times when THEY were the life and soul of the party and their partners took a back seat. Because what I often find is that each of us has the ability to be all things but often, when we get into relationships, we decide what we are going to own in that relationship and what we are going to delegate for the other person to own. And as the other person takes ownership, over time, we start to believe that we no longer have it and this is a distortion of the truth.

Healing Action Step

Own the truth of who you are

Sit somewhere quiet (where you know you will not be disturbed) and reflect back on your relationship:

• Make a list of all the qualities that you perceive as having walked out the door (and out of your life) with your partner when he left.

• Next to each item, go back through your entire relationship and find all the times in the relationship that you achieved the exact same thing. Please note that it may not be that you did it in exactly the same way - you most likely did it in your own way. If he often got work promotions, look at where you were "promoted", perhaps in school committees, in the eyes of your family or within your social circles.

Completing this exercise thoroughly will help you to recognise that you possess each of the qualities that you miss in your partner to an equal degree, but in your own unique way.

Now, look at all the things you achieved while you were in the relationship that did not involve input from your partner.

• Write down all the things you achieved at work, within the family, socially, study courses, holidays you organized, etc.

• Go back to the times when you used your organizational skills, your likeability and your know-how to get things done.

• Keep going until you can clearly see you have buckets of

value and are absolutely able to achieve things on your own.

• Ideally you will have between 35 and 75 things listed. If you haven't, keep looking until you realise your mountain of value!

Review these lists regularly to remind yourself of your innate value and use your wheel of life to expand the full recognition of your achievements in every area of your life.

Step Two: Don't fantasize the relationship

It's human nature to find fault with people and situations, especially those closest to you but then, when they are gone, to forget those faults and remember only the good things about them. This psychological pattern that has its roots anchored in our deepest desire to have our personal preferences met by those closest to us. It causes a lot of unrealistic expectations and suffering in relationships and also creates narcissistic tendencies that cause many to take more than they are willing to give.

If you find yourself fantasizing about how wonderful the relationship was, regardless of whether or not you feel it was the right one for you, it's time to take a more balanced look. Until you can bring the good and bad qualities, the likes and dislikes, into some kind of balance in your mind, what you're actually doing is seeing that person through rose-tinted glasses. Of course, this works the opposite way as well. If all you can see are the bad qualities and your dislikes and you can barely acknowledge the good, you're seeing them through a veil of negativity.

Healing Action Step

Getting the good and the bad into perspective

Using your journal:

• Make a list of all the things that you like about your ex, all the qualities you admire that he brought to the relationship.

• Now make another list of all the things you dislike about your ex and all the ways in which you feel he inhibited the relationship.

• You need to bring that list to balance. For example, if there are thirty things you like and twenty things you dislike, you'll need to dig deeper and keep writing until you get that list to 30/30.

For every action there is an equal and opposite reaction and until you can find the balance, your view of your ex is distorted, causing you to remain in an emotional flux. You will convince yourself that you are incomplete and missing out on something just because that person is no longer in your life.

Attaining a balanced perspective will liberate your mind and dissolve painful emotions!

Whenever you feel you may be slipping backwards emotionally, you can come back to this list and expand it as more and more unconscious memories surface.

Step Three: Don't fantasize his new life

The next mistake made by many women whose partners have left them, either for someone else or for a more successful career is that they immediately and powerfully conclude that they are not good enough and begin fantasizing the amazing new life that their ex is about to live with his new partner or job.

If you're doing that, stop it right now! This is a powerful distortion that will devastate you if you allow yourself to continue doing it for too long. How do I know? Because I did it myself and it was one of the darkest, deepest and most unnecessary holes I dug for myself. And the distorted conclusions that I did make back then couldn't have been further away from how it actually turned out.

You may find that in your anger you are focused on the sacrifices *you* made throughout the relationship. Again, I encourage you to stop right now. Remember that we only make sacrifices when our needs are being met on some level. People rarely do things against their own will. It's healthy to bear in mind that your ex also made sacrifices for the relationship.

At the heart of issues that surround feelings of self-sacrifice, we usually find a lot of fear. Fear of finance, fear of ageing, fear of whether we really feel we have what it takes to start again and fear of finding love again. These are the reasons so many women stay in dead-end relationships and keep 'making sacrifices' – because aspects of the relationship are fulfilling needs driven by their personal insecurities.

Healing Action Step

Nobody is better off than anyone else

I must stress that this exercise is not to be dwelled upon as a vengeful exercise and it's often helpful to review it with a trusted friend – one who is able to help you keep the balance and be objective. This exercise will help you take a realistic view if you are fantasizing his life to an extent that is preventing you from moving forward.

• Sit quietly and, for a few minutes, imagine taking all the fear you feel and putting it in a small box next to you.

• Now, take a realistic look at what your ex has chosen to leave you for – it may be a job, another woman, or anything else.

• Using the areas defined in the Wheel of Life, identify all the disadvantages your ex may well experience now that he has chosen this new path. Look into every area – finances, friends, career, physical life, and so on.

• Keep going around the wheel, get into the detail as much as you need too without turning this into an exercise where you begin to imagine that you are somehow better than him. Just keep it real and keep the balance.

There is a divine order that is maintained throughout the universe and throughout nature. Nobody wins and nobody loses. But everyone transforms - it's a natural part of evolution.

Step Four: Ditch the ageist myth

This has to be the number one fear of middle-aged women going through a divorce. They fear that they are too old to:

…meet someone new

…build a secure financial future

…get back into the job market

…meet new people

…take up a form of study

…get back into shape

…and so on, and so on

With the retirement age for women set to exceed age 65 in the near future and with the general life expectancy continually increasing, it's clear to see that women in their 60s today are more the equivalent of women in their 40s only a few decades ago.

I hear so many women despair that we live in a world where youth and beauty are revered by the masses, particularly by men. Come on ladies, we need to get this one straight! How on earth can we buy into a paradigm of youth that lasts for roughly seventeen years (age eighteen to thirty five) in a lifetime that spans an average of eighty to ninety years!

It's ironic that, as young girls, we cannot wait to be all grown up, then we enjoy a "prime" that lasts about halfway into our thirties. After that we spend the rest of our lives (and the majority of our lives) trying to stay looking that way in order to feel desirable. This is a ridiculous paradigm and in many ways, as women, I feel we enable ourselves to be treated in this ageist way by buying into this lie.

Taking the time to look your best each day is an act of self-nurturing. I love taking care of myself. But when all the emphasis is on appearance and none on the value we hold within, we soon discover that we have a problem with ageing as we begin to define ourselves, and our worth, accordingly. We then fail to attract the types of men who are more concerned with inner beauty, instead attracting those more focused on outer beauty. I have literally asked hundreds of men whether they would prefer a woman who is gorgeous to look at but who has little inner beauty to a woman who is average looking but filled with inner radiance and confidence. Apart from the obviously shallow men who I knew would answer that question in the obvious way, the vast majority of men answered that they would prefer a woman who is confident and beautiful on the inside.

Age is irrelevant when it comes to love. Attitude is everything. It has been proven over and over again that the human brain only stops developing because we choose to stop learning, regardless of age. The moment we begin to learn again, neurons in the brain fire new synaptic connections, expanding our neural pathways and mental capacity. There is absolutely no reason why, at any age, we cannot continue our learning, other than our own self-induced fear that we are too old or redundant in society. If you are holding on to these types of beliefs, I strongly suggest that you add some new affirmations to your Creation Statement collection and start thinking differently. Remember that your life can only soar as high as your highest thought about yourself.

Here is a new affirmation that you may want to use if you are finding you have issues in this area:

My mind is eternally youthful and I am open to learning something new each day.

Speak only encouraging words to yourself, tell yourself you can and don't share your fears and concerns with others. If others project their fears onto you, politely and calmly state your own views or just let their comments go over your head. That is no longer your reality. Whether you are thirty or sixty, you still have so much more to learn and to give.

Set goals for the next decade and I assure you that your passion for life will return and begin to yield results that will amaze you. Get inspired and focus on building your inner radiance. Establish true connection with yourself and with others. You can start now or continue to wait around for circumstances to be ideal. Here's the secret– they will never be ideal - circumstances only become ideal because you make them so. It's your life and your choice and it would be a crying shame to waste another minute of it.

Healing Action Step

Own your own fountain of eternal youth

• Sit quietly and close your eyes. Take a couple of long, deep and relaxing breaths.

• Using your imagination, fast forward your life until you reach the last day - the day you are going to die. Really connect with what it feels like to be in that moment where you are just about to pass on from this world.

• Take as long as you need. Notice the detail, how you are feeling, whether you are peaceful and where you are.

• Now look back over your life from that place. Is there anything you wish you had done, or done differently? Anyone you wish you had spoken to? Any goal you wish you had taken the trouble to achieve? What legacy are you leaving behind for your children, your family, your partner or within the sphere of your work?

• Really connect with this moment and the details contained within it.

• Have as much of a conversation with your older self in that moment as you can and when you are ready, take a couple of deep breaths and come back into the room.

• Write down any impressions you gained, goals that were unrealised, people you wish you had cleared the air with or things you wish you had done (or done differently).

You now have a second chance to make all these things happen. Go take on the rest of your life!

Step Five: Stay focused on your new life

Make sure that you keep the vision of the way that you want your new life to look (as completed in your Wheel of Life) somewhere where you can see it everyday. Treat it as a living entity, keep breathing life into it and adapting it and stay focused on all the wonderful new things you want to create for your life. You know it may not be easy at times, but you also know it will be worth it so keep your attention focused.

Your attention and focus is only ever in one of three places:

❀ In the past (your memories).

❀ In the present (the present moment).

❀ In the future (your imaginings).

Ironically, as much as we love to live in the past and the future, the only true point of power from which we can ever create, is the present. Neither the past nor the future, are real in terms of creative power. The past is forever gone and the future is forever in the distance. Time and energy spent dwelling on past memories and future imaginings merely rob you of your creative power and focus. All we really ever have, or participate in, is the present moment. The more you keep your attention, focus and awareness in the present, the more peaceful you will feel overall.

Reflections:

How much energy would you free up if you kept your awareness in the present moment?

How much more could you accomplish with all this additional energy?

Step Six: Limit negative self-talk

You are who you say you are. The words you use are a powerful force. They reveal your attitudes and beliefs about yourself and your life. If you catch yourself using phrases like, "I can't" or "it's too hard" or "I hate…" or "I should" or "I can't stand" or any similar negative self-talk, then pay attention. You may barely even notice on a day-to-day basis the many ways in which your language is limiting you, restricting your capabilities. As the old saying goes - if you say you can't , then you can't!

If you are serious about believing in yourself and changing your life, you will not be able to move to great heights while you allow this type of limiting language to negatively impact your potential.

What you think, say and do are the three driving forces that direct your life. Not only do you need to be thinking, speaking and acting responsibly and lovingly towards yourself, you also need to use these three profound forces together to create your future. That means that each day you need to think about, speak about and act upon your aspirations.

Even if you think you're worthy and communicate that worthiness to others, but then fail to take the kind of action that puts your own priorities first - you will still fail to bring about the desired results. If these three driving forces – thought, word and deed - are not perfectly authentic and aligned you will continue to chase your tail in circles until you can truly think, speak and act unanimously in the direction of your dreams.

Reflections:

How many times a day do you notice yourself thinking thoughts of doom and gloom or speaking badly about yourself or your situation?

Are you willing to commit to making a different choice?

Here is another helpful affirmation that you can use to shift your focus in this area:

I am an empowered woman and I radiate this to the world. I take full ownership of my life, my relationships, my ideas, my choices and the direction my life is now taking. I know that I can't control others but I can control myself.

Step Seven: Keep expressing yourself

You may find that you need to express yourself (with others or in your journal) a lot more on some days, than others. Or you may, on some days, feel the need for more aggressive forms of exercise perhaps even punching some pillows if you have a lot of frustration that needs releasing. This is all perfectly normal and healthy - just keep the feelings flowing. If at times you feel surrounded by emptiness, then allow that emptiness to surround you and surrender to it. Make peace with being in your own energy and your own company and start taking up activities that you used to enjoy and that express your individual nature. Get re-acquainted with your likes and your dislikes and who you are as a person.

Reflections:

Are you journaling regularly about how you are feeling? What new insights are you gaining?

What are some of your most treasured activities from the past that you would love to take up again?

Step Eight: Keep it amicable

Parting with your ex as amicably as possible and maintaining a degree of friendship in the future, although sometimes unrealistic, is a very healthy thing. Initially you will need time away from each other but if you have children, developing this type of relationship becomes an absolute necessity. One of the most challenging things for divorced parents is to be able to share their children with their ex partner without speaking badly about each other in the children's presence.

Children, and especially young children, have a built-in self-blaming mechanism when it comes to things going wrong with their parents. When couples split up, the innate reaction of a young child is to feel that they did something wrong or that it is somehow their fault. This is enough of an issue to deal with on its own but you need to bear in mind that your child's DNA is a combination of both you and your ex and that hearing anything bad from either side makes a part of that child feel that it is unacceptable or unlovable. It's essential to refrain from having adult conversations or arguments in front of children who do not have the emotional skills to process what's happening.

Vicky's story...

Vicky was naturally devastated when her long-term relationship of six years broke up. She found it particularly difficult to hold it together in front of her four year old son, Max - the most adorable gift to come out of the relationship. Vicky was determined that Max would not be exposed to all the hurt and upset that she felt after the breakup and so she explained, in an age-appropriate way, that she would no longer be living with Max's dad. She arranged for Max to stay with his grandparents for a couple of days while she worked at pulling herself and her environment together as best she could.

Since she was emotionally unable to speak to Max's dad, she wrote a very gracious letter in which she expressed her hope that he would not speak badly of her or their situation to their son. She ensured that she only allowed herself time to be upset when Max was asleep and she was alone with her journal or with her friends and family. At first, unfortunately, Max's dad chose to vent the odd comment to Max, which Max then repeated back to Vicky. She responded by doing the exact opposite - saying only good things about his dad. This seemed to calm Max and make him smile. The more Vicky worked through her emotions following the breakup, releasing her frustrations and heartache, the more she started to feel real gratitude towards her situation and the more genuinely great things she had to say to Max about his dad.

After about three months, Max came home one day and told Vicky that his dad had said she was the best mummy in the world. Vicky settled Max down with a colouring book, went into the bathroom and shed tears of relief. She had held firm to her belief and her vision for her son and somehow, that alone, had started to turn the situation around completely.

If you handle this time ethically and take full responsibility for your own healing, not only will you gain the respect of your ex but you will also be setting a positive example for your children on how to cope with crisis in future.

If your ex is not willing to amicably do what's in the best interest of your children, I highly recommend you find a good counsellor to help your children through this time.

Reflections:

Are you communicating with your ex, in front of your children, in a way that does not stress them when they are present?

Do you catch yourself saying bad things to your children about your ex? Can you make a decision today to stopping doing this?

Step Nine: Missing the closeness and reaching out

One area that I have not yet addressed is that of genuinely missing your ex partner. Missing their arms around you. Missing their voice on the other end of the phone each day. Missing the little ways in which they were consistently a part of your day.

My best advice on this would be for you to find a suitable way of providing, to yourself, all the things that you feel you are missing each day. At night, sleep with the family pet, purchase a big new teddy bear or sleep with a pillow that you find comforting. If you are missing phone calls during the day, ask some of your friends if you can call them more frequently. If you are craving touch, schedule in regular massage and share hugs with your friends, family and children as much as possible. Whenever one of my best friends in the world, Julia, visits from abroad, she hugs me and holds me until she can feel that "the love tank" has been sufficiently filled up. I love her so much for that - it's one of my favourite things about her.

I am a strong believer that, when you are in a state of total despair, one of the best things you can do to uplift yourself is to give exactly the thing you need to someone else. If you need love, give love. If you need support, give support. Help a neighbour. Help someone else in need (though not in a way that creates dependency). Look around - the world is absolutely bursting with people that would appreciate a helping hand, a kind heart and a warm smile. I have always found, in my greatest moments of darkness, that helping someone else lifted me right out of the dark place I was in. All of a sudden you realise that you have so much left to give and that you do make a difference. You experience, first hand, the wonderful ways in which you are a gift to the world by the very nature of being alive.

Reflections:

What one thing can you think of right now that you are missing from your ex?

What step can you take today to give that to yourself without involving your ex?

Step Ten: Get closure and break your wedding vows

If you haven't yet written your letter of release to your ex (instructions on this can be found in the Emotional Journaling section in Chapter One), now is definitely the time. Remember that you are not actually going to send this letter or have anyone else look at it - this is purely an exercise in emotional release.

Just as you joined your lives together through the promises made in your wedding vows or the promises you made when you embarked on a long-term relationship, you now need to separate your lives and make a clean energetic break.

Before you complete the vow break, it is particularly important that you have expressed all remaining bottled up feelings by writing that letter of release to your ex. You need to get everything completely off your chest. Please don't embark on the Vow Break without doing that first, otherwise it will not feel complete. If you have written the letter, retrieve it right now and read the letter out loud with the intention of letting go. Please ensure that you are not feeling angry or vengeful - if you are, stop the exercise and do more writing in your letter. Get all of those emotions out! You should be in a fairly neutral space when you do this exercise.

Healing Action Step

The Vow Break

Note that it may help if you ask a friend that you trust to help you complete this exercise by reading the words and guiding you into the space, then getting you to repeat the vow break after them once you get to that part of the exercise.

When you are ready, go into a quiet space where you know you will not be disturbed and complete the following:

1. Close your eyes and take a couple of deep, calming breaths.

2. Imagine you are in a setting that is perfect for breaking your wedding vows, whatever setting comes to mind and seems perfectly appropriate.

3. Picture your ex standing in front of you and look straight into his eyes.

4. Hold the connection energetically, open your eyes and read the following out loud, with connection and feeling, filling in the blank spaces using each other's names.

The Vow Break

I _____ release you _____
as my husband/partner in life. I thank you for the time and
the life that we have shared. I understand that the love we
have shared, lives on as a beautiful eternal bond, but that our
relationship in the physical here and now has transformed for
the highest good of both of us. I release you to your destiny
as I now reclaim the wholeness of who I am. I am free and you
are free.

_____

[Signed by You]

Close your eyes and imagine your energies separating and release him into the distance.

Don't underestimate the power of this exercise. On some level,
your ex will pick up the energy of what has happened, almost immediately, and may even respond by getting in touch as he feels
the energetic shift and tries to fathom what is happening. Don't
let any of that concern you. Most importantly stay in your own
energy and your own individuality and make any adjustments
that you feel you need to make in your own life to move forward.

Five important tools to help you move forward

Sometimes it helps to remember that there is always someone in
the world that is worse off than you. Use your gratitude journal
daily and give thanks for all the many things you do have. Continue to expand your gratitude on a daily basis.

These will always be your most powerful tools going forward:

- **Get things into perspective.** Neither one of you is better off than the other here, regardless of how it seems. Release your ex to his own thoughts, words and actions. Take full ownership of your emotions, your life and yourself and allow him to do the same. No more pointing fingers.

- **Give yourself all the things that you feel you are missing** since he left and allow others to step in and participate as well.

- **Use the new vision you hold for your life** (as laid out in your Wheel of Life) to guide you. Speak positively about your future.

- **Learn to love being in your own company again.** Become your own best friend and reassure yourself. Take up interests that reflect your individuality.

- **Focus on what you have** instead of what you don't have, particularly when you're feeling low.

Don't worry if you still have any fears and doubts about your future - we are going there next!

Chapter 5

Facing your Fears

"No matter what you've been told, what you've experienced or what you believe – you always have the power to change it."

– Desiree Marie Leedo –

The next part of our journey is concerned with dissolving fear of the future. It's interesting to note that you will only feel fear in the areas of your life in which you currently hold little or no power. Therefore, fear is a direct invitation to transform something that's not working for you.

Fear is a crippling emotion. It is the mind playing out all sorts of worst-case scenarios, while simultaneously attempting to integrate possible outcomes in a way that makes as much sense as possible. It's like a complex game of chess that won't allow you to rest until you find the perfect move.

After divorce, some women face a lot of fear in the area of finance and career, especially if their ex-partners provided secure foundations in these areas. On the other hand, women who are successful in these arenas, often face different fears involving their physical, social and family arenas. They can easily get roped into feelings of guilt around seeing their ex suffer and may unfairly continue to support them financially, even when it was their ex who wanted out of the relationship.

Dealing with fear can be torturous, keeping you awake well into the night while your mind struggles to find the perfect solution amidst all the change you are facing.

We have already looked at how divorce or separation rapidly shifts your foundations and priorities, creating a major identity crisis as you transition from who you were to who you are now becoming. We know that this is normal and even necessary, that is, provided you don't get stuck in this phase of the process.

So what is fear?

There are two types of fear. The first is *adaptive fear* - the type that is healthy, helping us cope with transition and keeping us alert and alive. The second is *maladaptive fear* – the type developed by undergoing a traumatic experience that makes living and enjoying life afterwards really difficult. In this chapter we will be working to ensure that you do not develop *maladaptive* fear in response to your current experience.

My favourite definition of fear is from Neale Donald Walsch, who wrote the book "Conversations with God". He describes fear with the following acronym:

False
Evidence
Appearing
Real

The human brain is designed to detect fear and respond accordingly – it does this to protect us. We know this is perfectly normal and we rely on this to keep us safe in times of danger. When primitive man was confronted with surviving the wrath of wild animals, the natural elements and other daily life threatening situations, he relied on the "fight or flight" response to keep him alive.

Although we have evolved way beyond that and, subsequently our brains have evolved to more sophisticated levels of reasoning, we still cannot fully escape reverting back to this primitive response when confronted with stressful situations that we perceive as threatening. In an instant, clear thinking goes out the window and we revert right back to this innate stress-response.

When you are in a state of fear, you are imagining that there are more harmful than helpful experiences that await you in the future. Your brain does not know the difference between what is real and what is imagined. It simply responds to your perception by flooding your system with stress hormones while your mind works around the clock to find a solution that will keep you safe.

Reflections:

 Look back at your Wheel of Life empowerment audit - can you identify the fears you are attached to relating to those bottom three areas?

Eradicating fear

It's important that we balance your perception of the future otherwise you will feel paralysed in moving forward to greet it. Scaring yourself half to death with worry is futile and it makes more sense to cultivate a healthy state of mind around what it is you fear.

Take a moment to think back to difficult times you've been through in the past. Do you remember some of your worst fears that accompanied them? Would it be true to say that many of those fears never actually materialised?

Fear can cause us to bury our heads in the sand, engage all sorts of delay tactics and create additional dramas. And while there is nothing anyone can really give you that will entirely eradicate the fear you feel, I want you to know that this is a good thing! A dominant and overpowering sense of fear is definitely unhealthy but a small amount of uncertainty will keep you humble, willing to learn and change. It will encourage you to remain open to the guidance and assistance of others who want to see you succeed on your journey.

Catherine's story...

Catherine was absolutely terrified of returning to work after her separation. She had been out of the corporate world for nine years and had since only run a small hobby business from home - something to keep her busy while her husband travelled away much of the time.

Although they had no children, after their separation there simply wasn't enough money left to sustain her through any type of maintenance plan and she decided to return to the only career she had known before – as a supervisor in the retail sector. When Catherine came to see me she was so afraid she could barely sleep, and the fear kept her stomach knotted in tension. She feared that her skills had become redundant with the passage of time and felt intimidated by successful people in general.

We made a list of all the tasks Catherine would need to undertake before she could get back to work and flagged up the skills that needed updating. Her software and team leadership skills needed revisiting. I encouraged Catherine to include the skills she had used in her small home business over the last ten years in her CV, something that hadn't really occurred to her at that point. By the time she was done updating her CV she realised that she had even more skills to offer than she had when she had first worked in retail and that she could use these new skills to fast track her career and increase her wages much faster than she would have if she hadn't developed them.

She took a short software training and communication skills course before enrolling with a couple of recruitment agencies. When she landed her first position, Catherine returned to see me so that she could address the fear she felt about tackling her dreaded first day back at work. We put together a ridiculously simple checklist to help her deal with all the unknowns, starting with the moment she woke up and ending at the close of her first day. It went as follows:

Catherine's Checklist: Answer yes or no and address any "no's" as thoroughly as possible. Do you know how to…?

❀ *Wake up to an alarm clock?*

❀ *Get ready to leave in time?*

❀ *Park your car at the station?*

❀ *Get the train to the city?*

❀ *Navigate to your new place of work?*

❀ *Introduce yourself to your point of contact when you first arrive and make light conversation?*

❀ *Make yourself at home at your new workstation?*

❀ *Operate the technological equipment?*

❀ *Use the phone or ask for instruction on how to operate the phone?*

❀ *Communicate effectively with other staff members?*

❀ *Attend a meeting, introduce yourself and invite others to introduce themselves?*

❀ *Find yourself lunch at a nearby café at lunchtime?*

❀ *Find your way back to the station after work?*

❀ *Get the train back home?*

❀ *Be able to do it all again tomorrow based on all the additional skills and assurance you have gained today?*

As I said, this was a ridiculously simple exercise but Catherine was an extreme worrier and it gave her the support and reassurance she needed to get a great night's rest, safe in the knowledge that she could confidently tackle every aspect of her first day.

    Within six months of being back at work Catherine was offered two new positions, both promotions from her starting role, and both with far better wages. She had continued to confront her fears and apply herself and it had paid off fast. Today she is pleased that she took action and tackled things head on, even though she had felt so terrified at the time. She has made many new friends at work and is fast tracking her way to a whole new career and a self-fulfilled new life. But best of all, for the first time in years, Catherine feels strong. And when I ask her now if she would rather be in the life she was living before or the one she's now created - she says she wouldn't trade the life she has now for anything in the world. She loves who she has become and refuses to live with fear.

The only way to truly eradicate fear is to take action. That's it. Yes, it requires a little courage but let's face it – if you don't develop some courage, you won't get very far in creating an empowered life. It may help to remember that life will never give you more than you can handle. It really helps if you can trust that.

Five common fears and what to do about them

Here is a list of the five most common fears shared by women who are confronting change through divorce or separation:

1. I've lost my financial security and I'm afraid of what the future holds.

I question whether financial security is something that really exists. When we are struggling to make ends meet, we fear that we will never have enough. But, equally, when we gather ample money, we fear that we will somehow lose it. Millionaires, who need to maintain a high standard of living, constantly strategise the loss of their wealth and readily admit to the same fears about money, and future security, as those struggling to make ends meet.

Building savings and financial assets towards retirement are absolutely crucial, but if you find yourself in a situation where suddenly you can barely make ends meet then, again, you need to confront this fear. You will need to set goals and create an action plan for change and keep placing one foot in front of the other as you work towards it. You will never get a different result tomorrow by applying the strategies that got you to where you are today. You must initiate some kind of change.

Audit your career skills and identify how you can apply them differently so that you maximise opportunities for increasing your finances. As soon as possible, begin to factor in saving regularly, no matter how small.

If you are feeling desperate and unhappy in any other area of your life, you are devaluing yourself by refusing to implement healthy change. You may also be allowing others to devalue you. Take whatever steps are necessary to create a more enriching experience and remember that it's the small decisions you make day-to-day that shape the direction of your life. Not deciding or inaction is also a decision.

Another fear that some women face after divorce, particularly if they have very few assets as a result of the breakup, is that they have nothing to offer a potential new partner financially. Here we must introduce and understand the concept of fair exchange of resources that occurs in relationships.

A husband who does well at work often does so because his wife takes ownership of the household responsibilities in his absence, thus freeing up his time and providing support in a way that enables him to perform optimally in this arena. And the wife, who frustrates her husband because she does not like cooking, may be the one organising the household finances and paperwork (including his business paperwork) because he doesn't like to do it himself. Couples come together because they understand, at a deep level, that they are a good fit for their preferred exchange of resources and that their priorities and needs will be met in this way - whether they are physical, mental or emotional.

If you cannot recognise your innate value and the value that you bring to a relationship (or the world at large), you may continue to define your self-worth in financial terms only. You will then attract the types of partners who will happily reflect this lack of belief in yourself back to you.

Marie's story...

After her divorce, Marie dated a man who was adamant that all the finances should be split down the middle. That's a fair agreement to establish within a relationship but in this case it meant that he never treated her to dinner or bought her anything, even though she spoiled him using what little financial resources she had. She cared for him when he was ill, spent much of her time driving over to his home and was constantly fitting her schedule around his. In the beginning she thought that he was just making a point, but as the relationship progressed Marie realised that this man didn't even want to have children because he didn't like the idea of supporting a family financially, even though he had a very well paid job.

The shocking realisation that they would never be able to work as a team financially slowly sunk in. Because she was dating him around the same time that she was starting to re-build her life, and she was struggling to make ends meet, it wasn't long before he started complaining that she was holding him back from things he wanted to do - like attending concerts and go away on weekend breaks.

Even though this man was earning six times what Marie made, he still refused to pay for her accompanying ticket for a concert he wanted them both to attend! By the time she came to see me she felt totally inadequate and her self-esteem had taken a massive knockl. In our sessions, she woke up and realised how small, afraid and in-adequate HE was. She also realised that she had met him at a time when her own self-esteem was on the floor and that he had come in as a direct reflection of her own inner issues around feeling inadequate due to finances.

If you find yourself anywhere near a situation like this, now or in the future, my best advice is to get out, as fast as you can!

Being honest and up front about who you are and where you are currently positioned in life, no matter where or what that is, is all that is ever required of you. If someone can't accept that or support you in that, they really aren't the right person for you to be around at that particular time. You are in control and it is up to you decide what you will and will not accept in your life.

Reflections:

What steps can you take to increase your income and when will you start?

Can you recognise your unique inner value and your contribution within relationships outside of your finances?

2. I'm too old or unattractive to find love again

I briefly touched on a related fear in the previous chapter relating to "Ditching The Ageist Myth". Many of my clients also have a distinct fear about their age, purely from a physical point of view. When they complete their Wheel of Life audit and come to the Physical Well-Being area, they realise that they feel tired, washed out, frumpy and out of shape. They wonder where they will find the time and the energy to cope with all the changes they have to confront and they feel great despair about their romantic prospects for the future.

I've already mentioned the heavy emphasis society places on physical appearance and how youth and physicality are revered, while inner qualities come off a poor second. But, as I said before, the majority of real men prefer qualities of inner confidence and radiance. When you are in love with yourself and with your life, you radiate a quality that is beautiful to behold and irresistible to those around you.

I do believe that there is great benefit to be gained in maintaining a healthy body weight purely because it gives you the vitality and longevity required to fully enjoy your life. This includes being over-weight or under-weight as both will leave you feeling lethargic and cause serious health issues over time. Outside of that, all that is left for you to do is to love and accept who you are - as you are - so that others can do the same.

To alleviate this fear, spend time each day looking into your eyes in the mirror, repeating the following Creation Statements to yourself (you can alternate them if required):

I love and accept you (your name). You are perfect just as you are.

I accept you (your name), exactly as you are. You are timeless. I love you whether you think you are failing or whether you think you are succeeding. I love you exactly as you are.

Be realistic - if you feel you want to shed or gain some weight, create an action plan for doing this. Take up a new class, maintain healthy eating habits, visit a physician or nutritionist and make the necessary changes. If you would like to update your hairstyle or your dress style, have a makeover and get more in touch with your feminine side so that you can begin to enjoy your relationship with your body again. But don't fall into the trap of believing that you are unattractive because you are not a certain age or shape.

Choose to be beautiful at every age and watch the world around you reflect that back to you.

Reflections:

Is there anything you would like to change about your style or your appearance? When will you do it?

Are you willing to love and appreciate yourself for who you are today?

3. I'm afraid of being rejected by family members or mutual friends

It's true that family members and mutual friends often take sides after a breakup. This is something that you will have to accept even though it can be extremely hurtful when you discover that people who you have built a close bond with over time, suddenly decide to turn against you or, even worse, cut you out of their lives altogether.

Know that, with the passing of time, some may come around, get back in touch and work out the basis for developing a new individual relationship with you. If they do, that's wonderful, provided you would genuinely like to take that relationship forward into your future. But if they don't, all it means is that they are not a part of the new journey you are about to embark on. Let them go.

Patricia's story...

Patricia had a strict religious upbringing and when her marriage of twelve years ended, her own family, instead of offering their support, judged her and took sides with her ex who was trying to hold the marriage together, despite having cheated on her. Patricia felt it was a double blow, particularly as her ex's family took sides against her as well. She tried to maintain a relationship with both families but soon found herself feeling more and more broken with each passing bit of contact.

By the time she came to see me her guilt and self-loathing had almost destroyed her. Although she felt humiliated and betrayed by her husband's actions, she had begun to convince herself that she was a bad person for not wanting to stay in the marriage and try to work it out. How could she? There was not a scratch of trust left, particularly with the way she felt he was playing up to her family, manipulating them through their religious beliefs to get the result that he wanted.

Patricia's struggle to let go was monumental. I asked her to identify the people in her life who showed the surrogate natural parental tendencies towards her that she felt she was missing from her own family. Then I encouraged her to go and spend time with those surrogate people and open up to them about what was happening. Being a very private person, she did not find this idea appealing at all but she agreed to follow my suggestion.

Within six weeks of opening up to these people, she started to gain a completely new understanding. She was getting all the support and acceptance that she felt she was lacking from her own family and she started to feel more at peace. She stopped struggling and remained distant from her family as she worked through her own feelings of acceptance towards herself and her situation.

After a couple of weeks, her family began to wonder why she wasn't getting in touch anymore and why she didn't appear to be quite so upset. Slowly, they started to move away from the manipulative behaviour of her ex, despite their initial disapproval.

Patricia never did heal the relationship with her ex's family but she did heal the one with her own. And in the process, she gained some deep new relationships with her "parental surrogates" – people who she now loves and treats as family as well.

If that makes you feel sad, hurt or disappointed, it may help to go back to your Wheel of Life. Look at your vision for all the areas of your life and then identify the ways in which these people would not fit into the new life you are about to create. Your world will continue to change in many ways and you will meet amazing new people anyway. Sometimes, there are relationships that just need to be left behind as part of the dead wood you need to cut from the tree of your life.

Say goodbye to those you are leaving behind. You can do this ceremoniously by closing your eyes and visualising the person standing in front of you. Look into their eyes, thank them for the time you have shared and the contributions you have made to each other's lives. Wish them well and set them free with love.

Reflections:

Is there anyone that you know you need to cut loose or say goodbye to?

Can you set them free with love?

4. My Children will grow up without their father

It can make you feel sad to know that your children will never share both parents together in the same way again. However, it's never a healthy situation for children to live in an environment where they are constantly exposed to tension and anxiety between their parents. From a very young age, children are learning how to interact as adults and they are learning this directly from both parents. They are learning how to interact with members of the opposite sex and in a stressful environment, fraught with tension and arguments, they are not exactly being exposed to two healthy role models.

It's far better for your children to share their time between your and your ex partner's homes than to be exposed to an environment that is emotionally toxic. If you're concerned about the effects of having less of a male presence around on a day-to-day basis, then look around and identify the other suitable male figures in your life.

Write a list of all the masculine qualities you think your children are missing now that your ex is no longer around and identify the male figures around you who are already taking that role upon their shoulders. Have them become more active in you and your children's lives - this could be a brother, cousin, grandfather or trusted male friend. Again, draw on your support network and ask for help as needed.

I usually encourage an amicable split where possible. However, if the breakup of your relationship has been acrimonious I must stress again that you DO NOT include any of your children in your own negative opinions about your ex or his behaviour. We touched on this in the previous chapter in the Ten Steps To Creating Emotional Balance under Step Eight - Keep it Amicable. You may want to go back and re-read the story of Vicky and Max.

In a quest for emotional revenge, many parents embark on this type of destructive behaviour in an attempt to keep their children on their side. You may feel like you want to hurt your ex, but in truth, you'll only be hurting your children.

This also applies to extended family. They need to agree not to share their opinions of the behaviour of either parent or make negative remarks in front of the children. There is no limit to the amount of chaos and damage done to children when this scenario plays out over days, months and even years.

Being disciplined about not making negative comments really is the only mature solution to giving children the best kind of care in a breakup situation. If you notice that they are having a difficult time adapting to all the change, again, it's imperative that you seek out an experienced professional who can support them and give them the right kind of care at this time.

Reflections:

Do you recognise yourself in any of the above scenarios?

What can you do today to create healthier interactions with your ex that will benefit your children?

5. I'm dependent and I don't know how to...

These are more transient fears and there are a myriad of ways for each woman to finish that sentence. While this may sound a little patronizing to some readers, it's surprising how many women out there have absolutely no idea of how to do many of the things their partners usually did for them. The list can be endless:

❁ pump the tyres or check the oil in the car.

❁ pay the bills.

❁ locate and manage paperwork relating to the mortgage and bank accounts.

❁ change a light bulb or plug.

❁ mow the lawn.

❁ paint or decorate a room.

❁ make the right financial investments.

❁ work out the value of their pensions.

❁ handle insurance policies.

…and so on and so on.

If any of these fears ring true for you, don't worry – this will pass quickly. These fears are easily overcome by taking appropriate action.

Healing Action Step

Taking Ownership of Physical Tasks

Start by making a list of everything that needs to be done and that you don't feel you have the necessary experience to handle.

- Identify the people in your life who can assist you by showing you how to complete these tasks yourself and then tackle each task on your list until you know exactly how to do it yourself.

- Search Google and You Tube - both are excellent resources for all kinds of practical tutorials and will help you understand what needs to be done so that you do not get ripped off should it be necessary to hire a handyman.

- Take ownership of your accounts and finances as well as the legal paperwork relating to every area of your life. Review, organise, categorize and file it all away together, keeping it in one place so that you always have it to hand when needed.

When you have successfully mastered or delegated each task on your list, you will have proved to yourself exactly how capable you really are and it will give you so much confidence!

Now that we've covered some of the common fears, let's look at what you can do when real fear starts to overwhelm you.

What to do when fear overwhelms you

The most important thing is to chunk it down into a do-able list of action steps. As you work through the list and tick off the items you will gain confidence and the feeling of overwhelm will disappear. With each small victory your fear will be minimized and your confidence will expand.

Be courageous and go for it. Draw on your support network if you need to - ask them to help you with planning your action steps or to support you while you take those actions yourself. But resist the temptation for them to take any action on your behalf! This is about you empowering your life and this is a profound way to set the ball rolling.

Healing Action Step

Clarifying the fear

Here are four useful steps for activating a powerful break-through when confronting your fears. Let's move through each of these steps one by one.

1. Identify, with absolutely clarity, exactly what your fears are.

- Write down a list of your fears, clarifying exactly what it is that you are afraid of.

- Now, for each item on the list, introduce the question "Why am I afraid of this?" For example, you may feel afraid of going back to work and, consequently, think that this is the main fear you are addressing, but by asking the question, "why am I afraid to go back to work?" you will produce a different set of responses that more closely reflect the deeper underlying fear.

Once you uncover that fear, you may notice that it keeps popping up in other areas of your life. You are then addressing a very different fear to the one you originally thought you had.

Dissolving these deeper fears will produce a far more profound result than attempting to deal with the fear that appeared on the surface.

2. Determine the action steps required to overcome your fears.

- Next to each fear, write down five to seven small action steps that you can take to overcome that particular fear.

- Once you have noted down the smaller action steps, if, you look at the fear and it still feels in any way overwhelming, look back at those five to seven action steps and chunk each of them down further by creating five smaller steps that will help you achieve each that step.

- Continue to chunk them down until you can clearly see a path for overcoming each aspect that makes up that fear. When you are done, you should feel confident that you know exactly what actions you need to take to overcome each fear on the list.

3. Take action!

Decide which of the smaller action steps you are going to tackle each day and schedule them in. Don't get distracted or delay them. As you slowly work your way through the list, you will gain momentum, find yourself feeling more capable and slowly conquer that fear.

4. **Focus on the outcome you want, not the outcome you don't want.**

Be disciplined and engage your mind as an ally, not an enemy. Remember that your mind will continue to look for the worst outcome in every situation in an attempt to protect you. Your job now is to re-direct your mind away from the worst outcome, and allow it to envision the new outcome you desire.

One of the best ways to do this is to stop yourself when you have a "doom and gloom" thought. Stop your mind right there in that moment and tell the thought that it is now redundant. Immediately follow that by stating the new desired outcome out loud. This is how you slowly train your mind to think in a different way.

For example:

Negative thought: I'll never find love again

Re-directed thought: I am an amazing woman with so much to offer and I choose to find real and lasting love.

Negative thought: I'm a failure, I've failed at my marriage and I'll never succeed on my own.

Re-directed thought: I trust the new direction that my life is taking. I've succeeded at many things and I will succeed at many more. I can achieve whatever I put my mind and my heart to.

Don't rob yourself of the opportunity to take full ownership when dealing with your fears and remember that they are not unique to you. There are thousands of women around the world - right now in this exact moment – who share the same fears as you do.

Have the courage to feel the fear

Understanding that these feelings are a natural reaction to what is occurring will help you put things into perspective.

The way to break through fear is to break down your inner resistance to change because what you resist, persists. On days when you're feeling low and your fears are getting the better of you, one of the best techniques for dealing with them is to invite them in and experience them with full intensity.

Healing Action Step

Invite in The Fear

- Close your eyes and call forth one of your greatest fears. Allow it to saturate every fibre of your being as you feel it with full intensity. When you are in the fear, locate any tangible feelings that may accompany it in your body (for example, a heavy feeling around your heart or a knotted feeling in your stomach).

- As you hold the fear with full intensity, you will notice that energetically, a space opens up and the fear seems to lessen. At this point, move your focus away from the fear and place it on the space that is opening up - it should feel a bit like freedom or relief. Feel this space as fully as possible and hold it for a few seconds.

- Now switch your focus again to the fear and invite it back with full intensity. You may notice that the intensity has lessened. Hold it for as long as feels comfortable and then switch your focus back to the small space that is still expanding and focus there for as long as possible.

- Continue to switch back and forth between the fear and the space that is opening up until you feel the fear dissipate.

If you complete this exercise properly you will find that the fear will truly dissolve the more you surrender and you will feel so much lighter.

You can also use the following Creation Statement throughout the day to help alleviate fear. Type it into your mobile phone and set a two hourly reminder if necessary:

I am willing to witness my fear. I am willing to make a different choice. I choose love.

And this sets the perfect scene for the start of our next chapter. Let's start activating some real self-esteem!

Phase Three

BUILDING YOUR STRONGEST LIFE

We are now into the final part of our journey together. This phase will guide you on how to powerfully invest your time and energy into building your strongest life. It will help you transform any lingering feelings of hopelessness regarding your future and enable true inner connection. Not only will you be empowered to build the life of your dreams, but you will also increase your own levels of personal power and self-esteem. With a little courage and inner optimism you can reach out and fully embrace the new life that awaits you.

Well done, you've come a long way now and it's important that you acknowledge all the great work you have been doing. If you've completed the exercises and have been using the recovery tools, you should be feeling much more balanced and on purpose, even a little excited about approaching the next steps.

Low self-esteem in women – a global epidemic

When I look around today I see a world filled with so many frightened and insecure women who are quietly going about their business, some of them in a lot of pain. Physically, they fear that they are ageing and that they don't measure up to the airbrushed images of women in the media. Emotionally, they're afraid of following their dreams - afraid of failing and some more afraid of success.

Despite the progress women have made in the world since the introduction of the female liberation movement, somehow we seem to have regressed with regards to our connection to our inner selves. More and more we have lost our sense of self-worth and our understanding of the true power of what it means to be female.

Looking at the upcoming generations, I see millions of young girls engaging the fairytale myth. These little girls grow up desperately wanting to be those princesses, so attracting strong and controlling partners who they think will protect them in life.

I see young teenage women strutting around in age-inappropriate clothing and make-up, desperately aspiring to imitate the idealistic and unrealistic airbrushed models that stare back at us from glossy pages and digital screens. These young women crave the validation that they associate with being sexy, desired and idolised by society and will go to all sorts of self-disrespecting lengths in their quest to obtain it. Too many young girls also aspire to be celebrities without any real understanding of the consequences accompanying this type of lifestyle.

I see young women in their late teens and early twenties who prioritise their boyfriends above their education choices and career paths. They fail to appreciate the lasting impact that these crucial decisions will have on the rest of their lives - decisions that need to be taken as young adults. So often they treat these crucial decisions about as casually as they would a choice about what dress to wear on a night out.

I see women in their thirties who are unhappy with their careers or marriages, yet so desperate to start a family as they are all too caught up in their ticking biological clocks. Some of them feel like their dreams are slowly slipping away yet they refuse to initiate change because of low self-esteem, fear of bad timing or an expanding lack of empowerment in an area of their lives. They keep hoping that things will get better but they refuse to take the necessary steps to make any change.

I see women in their forties, fifties and sixties stuck in dead-end marriages. Their dreams have almost completely died and they are disillusioned with their lot after giving up their own dreams to raise children who are now flying the nest to start lives of their own. They have lost their self-connection and their identity. They live quiet, miserable lives of desperation and they know they can't walk away because they have sacrificed their ability to be independent or resigned themselves to a life of martyrdom.

And I see the women who are going through divorce or separation. They are sad, afraid, disempowered and desperate to get their lives back on track but ironically these are the women who are really being given a second chance. Even though in the eye of the storm, it doesn't quite feel that way.

While I'm definitely not advocating that the above is true for every woman and I appreciate that every divorce situation is unique, it certainly is true of a large sector of society.

We are not taught as women, especially as young women, how to identify what empowerment looks like or how to fully take ownership of every aspect of our life. Therefore, it's not too surprising that, statistically speaking, women become more and more dissatisfied with their lives from the age of forty-five upwards. While, at this exact same age, men begin their upward trend of becoming more satisfied with their lives as they reach the peak of influence in their careers.

The Invisible Goddess – what does she look like?

The Invisible Goddess is anything but invisible. That's because the word **invisible** can also be interpreted as **in-visible** (visible within).

Being an empowered woman does not mean aspiring to be equal to a man or taking on the role of a man. While there are arguments on both sides of the coin, I believe that being an empowered woman means being a woman who is in touch with her femininity, her intuition and her ability to direct her life. It is her ability to radiate inner beauty and exemplify outer grace – much like a Goddess who exemplifies the following:

❀ She is self-confident and serene.

❀ She knows who she is. She knows her strengths and weaknesses and she is just as comfortable conversing with a beggar as she is with a king.

❀ She is warm and sensitive but no pushover.

❀ She is an inspired leader of the family and knows how to be a woman, allowing her man to step up and be a man.

❀ She takes responsibility for her own self-care, she is connected to her own dreams and takes ownership of achieving her goals.

❀ She is a positive influence on the world, sharing her wisdom with those around her.

❀ She knows how to handle herself confidently and protect what really matters to her.

❀ She lives a self-fulfilled life and people love to be around her.

❀ She never plays the sacrificial lamb and therefore doesn't blame others when things go wrong in her own life.

❀ She doesn't try to control others because she knows that the only person she can control is herself.

❀ If she notices something that she doesn't like in her own life she makes the necessary adjustments and re-directs her energy so as to affect change.

💮 She does this without complaining because she understands that she is a powerful creator with a profoundly intuitive guidance system and she knows that she is able to follow this and alter course whenever necessary.

I don't see a whole lot of this type of women in the world to-day. This is the change I am working so passionately to bring about - to remind every woman of the truth and beauty of her own unique soul.

Chapter 6

Activating Core
Self-Esteem

"If you're waiting for permission from someone else to be empowered, you're never going to get there."

— Desiree Marie Leedo —

Building a strong life requires a healthy connection between
your inner and outer self. While your outer self is expressed through the areas that make up your Wheel of
Life, your inner self is largely concerned with how you feel about
yourself on the inside. It relates to your overall sense of self-
worth and how this impacts the outer areas of your life.

In Chapter 3 you discovered the areas of your life in which
you gave away personal power. When we lack power in any area
of our lives, what we are really lacking is the *self-belief* that allows
us to hold power in that area - especially when we're coming
through relationships where our partners were holding the power
in certain areas for us.

Activating Core Self Esteem Within Your Wheel of Life

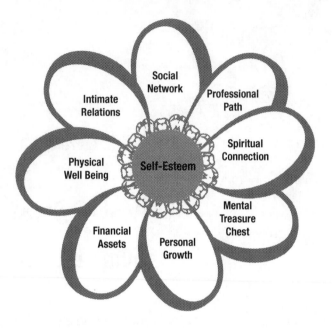

We understand that personal power needs to be raised in areas where it can be lacking but, without introducing self-esteem, it can be tempting to go down the road of doing just about anything to manipulate others or create further obstacles. We do this to avoid taking the necessary action because we don't want to confront challenge head on. It is only when we have true self-esteem that we can fully activate our personal power and make the kind of authentic choices that initiate powerful change. It's easy to see how self-esteem and personal power are an essential duo for building your strongest life.

In this chapter you will learn the secrets of building healthy inner self-esteem, and this will help you as you reclaim your true power from a place of integrity.

My Journey with self-esteem

On my own journey of healing and integration after the breakup of my marriage, the biggest challenge I faced was around the issue of self-esteem. I became determined never to let an outer event floor me in the same way ever again. I was even more determined to connect to my inner value and be able to express my worth authentically as a way of life.

Back then I didn't fully understand what self-esteem really was or how to engage it. To me it was just a term that was banded about in personal development seminars, referenced as an ability to hold oneself in enough esteem to be able to assert oneself with others in a way that they would clearly understand that if they didn't play ball or back down, there would be consequences. I've since come to understand that none of that is true self-esteem – it's just a coping mechanism for dealing with power struggles.

I came to discover that true and healthy self-esteem leads to authentic personal power like nothing else. Not the type of power that aggressively draws lines of defence or engages in manipulative power struggles. Or even the type that asserts one's ability to stand up and fight when others get in your space. That's playground self-esteem and has nothing to do with the real thing.

I'm talking about the kind of esteem that allows you to connect with your inner self and your innate purpose - the kind that comes from the depths of your soul and cries out for fearless expression. It's your connection to that little voice inside you that is always guiding and directing you about which way to go, which situations and which people to invite into your life and who to stay away from. It's the feeling in your gut that lets you know when you are making the wrong choice. It guides you with feelings of comfort and discomfort and it does this because it's a magnificently designed, built-in guidance system for navigating the path of your life.

Reflections:

What does the concept of self-esteem mean to you?

What kind of connection do you have to your own inner self-belief?

Why women find it challenging to build strong self-esteem

The reason so many women face great challenge when it comes to building a healthy sense of self-esteem is because:

- ❀ We are natural nurturers, prone to ignore that nagging feeling we get inside when we put the needs and desires of family members ahead of our own.

- ❀ We are natural peacemakers and will often do what is required to keep the peace in a situation, even if the outcome can be detrimental to us.

- ❀ We too readily accept that we are the ones who should make most of the sacrifices in order for our relationships to flourish.

- ❀ We often attempt to straddle two worlds, struggling to strike a balance between our natural instinct to be homemakers and our desire to forge our own identity.

Lack of knowledge creates fear. This is why so many of my clients who face the unknown are so afraid. When I work with a client for the very first time I know that her ability to hear me and work through my process effectively depends largely on her level of self-esteem. This is why I introduce the Wheel of Life so early on in my process. So many women have never sat down and identified, for themselves, where they are at and what it is they would really like to accomplish across all areas of their lives. When we complete this step in the process, an entire new world opens up for them and it's magic.

Throughout your life, people will come and go, jobs will come and go, circumstances will come and go, and even relationships will come and go. But the one thing that you are always stuck with is your life. It's worth ensuring it's a happy one because that's the only life you get to live.

What self-esteem is and what it isn't

Self-esteem is made up of a combination of beliefs, emotions and self-perception, which originates from a collection of childhood and adult life experiences. The way your family interacted with you when you were growing up and how you learnt to deal with challenges all played a critical part in developing the foundation of your self-esteem.

If you were spoilt as a child and were always allowed to have your own way at the expense of others, you will most likely have grown up with an inflated sense of self. Whereas, if you were talked down to as a child - told to be seen and not heard and generally reminded everyday that you are not worth much - you will have grown up with a deflated sense of self. Both scenarios will produce an individual with a distorted sense of self that falls into one of the following categories:

1. Those who believe they are always right and dismiss the opinions of others.

2. Those who believe they are always wrong and value the opinions of others above their own.

In truth, each one of us swings between these two extremes. We all encounter situations at times that cause us to beat ourselves up and, at other times, to beat others up. However, no matter where we are on the scale of emotion, fundamentally, we generally tend to be hard wired distinctly towards either one or the other.

True self-esteem is neither of the above. It's not connected to the successes or failures of any area of your life. It cannot be gained through the opinions of others, a good career, the adoration of a spouse, an inflated bank balance or anything else that exists outside of you.

True self-esteem is an innate connection to your authentic self. It is a deep inner belief in your own ability to be able to handle any situation you may find yourself in. It is a healthy acceptance and respect of self that commands respect from others without words needing to be exchanged.

Displaying this level of self-esteem is an energy that people can feel when they are in your presence. This level of self-belief creates a profound inner calm that radiates from within and magnetically draws others closer.

The difference between confidence and self-esteem

It's easy to confuse self-esteem with confidence but there really is a big difference between the two. Self-esteem is as intimately linked to self-knowledge as it is to self-belief, while confidence is associated with the acceptance and rejection of aspects of the self. Self-Esteem comes from integrating the self as a whole while confidence (and lack of confidence) compartmentalises the self into acceptable and unacceptable fragments.

For example, an actress who has true self-esteem may feel uncomfortable when asked to participate in a charitable sporting event because she knows she is ill equipped in this area. But, even knowing this, she still participates, giving her all to the best of her ability and has fun along the way, unafraid of looking silly or coming last.

Below are a few more points that will further illustrate the key differences between self-esteem and confidence:

Self-esteem	Confidence
Self-esteem is an *inner* sense of worth that prevents us from making submissive and disempowering choices. It distinctly relates to our relationship with self-belief - regardless of the changing scenery on the outside.	Confidence is influenced by what's happens on the *outside*. Each one of us is confident in areas of our lives in which we excel and, equally, each one of us lacks confidence in areas where we feel inadequate.
Self-esteem has an *intransient* presence that is reflected through every area of our lives, whether we feel confident in that area or not.	Confidence is more transient, it *comes and goes* to varying degrees throughout our lives. It is easily lost and gained, depending on outer performance.
Self-esteem understands and accepts the whole self as it is – the good and the bad.	Confidence accepts the good but rejects the bad, thereby fragmenting the self into what is and isn't acceptable.
Self-esteem understands and accepts each strength and weakness as valuable and essential in equal measure.	Confidence feeds on strength and tries to suppress weakness, thereby attempting to live a one-sided illusion that leads to unrealistic expectations.

The five cornerstones of self-esteem

Let's look a little closer at the cornerstones essential to creating true self-esteem:

1. **Self-esteem is an inside job:** there is no person, situation, circumstance, object or location outside of you that can give you a permanent or lasting sense of self-worth. This is a part of you that must be accessed from within by clarifying, acknowledging and appreciating your own magnificence and significant contribution to the world.

   If you depend on any person, event, financial status or organisation outside of you to define you at any level, you are opening yourself up to vulnerability and potential devastation in that area of your life.

   The truth is that anything outside of you that you find yourself overly relying on or using as a crutch for feeling good, will fail you at some point on the journey of your life. It's meant to. It's designed that way so that you can evolve an ever-greater connection with your own creative power.

2. **Self-esteem is the expression of your authentic self:** it requires constant attention to your personal priorities and self-perception. It demands that you place enough value on yourself to enjoy a relationship with yourself in which you can love, respect and value yourself unconditionally. It also demands that you create enough space in your life for the things that really matter to you, along with what matters to those with whom you share your life.

   This is not only about prioritising what really matters to you but also about engaging your inner guidance and self-belief in a way that allows you to bring it all to life.

3. **Self-esteem requires absolute acceptance of yourself as a whole:** this includes the parts of you that you perceive as good and bad. Any part of yourself that you try to reject will

pop up somewhere in your life, usually through another person, and continue to annoy you until you face it. Until you can see how every part of you is beneficial and vital to who you are and what you need to accomplish, you will continue to judge yourself and others.

Seeing yourself as a whole begins with identifying your strengths and weaknesses. You need to find the gifts in your weaknesses and take steps to multiply your strengths. You need to learn to catch and cradle the things that really inspire you and that make up the strong moments of your life instead of wasting energy resisting the experiences you don't really want. Why? Because, as we've already identified, what you focus on, expands.

4. **Self-esteem allows others to feel respected and accepted in your presence:** this leads to feelings of collaboration instead of separation. People with core self-esteem tend to focus on the best in others, not the worst.

Think about it, if you really believed in yourself, wouldn't you also believe in others? And if you were really in touch with the best of yourself, wouldn't you bring out the best in others? When we condemn others, it's usually a reflection of the way in which we condemn ourselves. This is because we refuse to fully accept parts of ourselves that we have been led to believe are "bad" or "unacceptable". This is an indication of poor self-esteem.

5. **Self-esteem requires no control or manipulation of people or events:** it takes responsibility for the self and the self, alone. It allows others the freedom to be who they are and do what they choose without trying to control their actions, and it makes decisions accordingly. Core self-esteem knows that we are never responsible for another and that we can never change or control another in any situation because the only person we can control or change is ourselves.

Remember, we cannot, nor should we try to, control the actions of someone else. Only our own. It's up to us to decide what is and isn't acceptable to us but it is not up to us to try and change someone else in an attempt to ensure that they fulfill our expectations. More about this in the next chapter on Personal Boundaries.

How self-blame can lower self-esteem

The issue of core self-esteem and its impact on the way we live our lives is becoming more and more of a challenge the world over. The spiritual paradigm of "we create our own reality" is now well established in our society and we hear about it all the time.

We witness the poor man carrying out kind deeds towards his fellow man, yet never seemingly able to make ends meet in his own life and we wonder why good people always suffer. Conversely, we watch the seemingly arrogant man getting ahead in life and we wonder why "not so nice people" get the spoils and rewards. But what we fail to see are the dominant, sometimes unconscious beliefs, at work beneath the surface of each of these individuals and how each is attracting an exact match to their internal ideas about who they are and what they are worth deep down inside.

When you go through a traumatic situation like divorce it's easy to slip into a cycle of self-blame by turning the paradigm "I create my own reality" in on yourself to the extent that it becomes self-destructive. This can cause you to embark on an endless journey of "self-fixing". I hope, by now, you understand enough to resist the urge to do this! I've seen countless women stuck in this pattern - rationalising that they are solely to blame for their partner leaving and that they brought this on themselves. They then punish themselves with self loathing.

The challenge here is largely due to the lack of understanding of how little of "creation" is done consciously and how much of it is done at an unconscious level. While we do participate in the creation of our lives and materialise our innermost dominant thoughts and beliefs, the "creation" that occurs as a result, consists of a *complex recipe* of thoughts, emotions, beliefs, experience and purpose that exist, mostly in the unconscious depths of our being. Therefore, it is an exercise in futility to conclude that you created this event consciously, merely by tapping into only one or two aspects of yourself.

There are some tools and techniques coming up a little later in this chapter that will begin to reveal some of your own *unconscious layers*. As the renowned Carl Jung once stated:

Until you make the unconscious conscious, it will continue to direct your life and you will call it fate.

Reflections:

Do you agree with the notion that we create our own reality?

Have you wanted to blame yourself for the breakup of your relationship because of things you think you consciously did or did not do?

How healthy is your core self-esteem?

Both personal power and self-esteem are living entities. Together, they are the force that you use to create your life. They are precious energies and the more you give them away, the less you have available to invest in yourself and your own life. Think of this as an energetic bank account. Every time you give your self-esteem away to someone else, you relinquish some of your personal power and fall into a degree of energetic deficit until, eventually, you feel so tired and drained that you are unable to use what's left to enjoy your own life.

The questions below are designed to get you thinking about how you really feel about yourself and your life and to look at the ways in which you negotiate your personal power in relationships.

1. Do you like yourself? Are you happy with the way you look, the way you interact with others and the way you feel about the general direction your life is taking?

2. Are you able to function optimally in relationships, both social and intimate, in a way that doesn't require that you control another person or in which you don't allow someone else to exercise control over you?

3. When you have a decision to make are you able to make it on your own without having it over-ridden by the opinions or approval of others?

4. Do you stand up for yourself in a calm and reasonable manner when facing confrontation?

5. Do you find yourself making decisions that pacify others when you know inside that's not the decision you really want to make?

6. Do you place too much importance on the ideas, opinions and decisions of others or change your behaviour to please another person?

7. Are you easily hurt, upset or prone to becoming reactive when someone says something negative to your or about you? And, if so, do you allow this to consume you for days on end, ultimately influencing your perception of yourself?

These questions are not designed to score you on your self-esteem but simply to allow you to begin to notice how you do or do not interact with yourself and others from a place of authentic self-worth.

Seven disciplines for developing healthy self-esteem

The good news is that low self-esteem can definitely be rectified. As you begin to build your new life after divorce or separation, your choice about whether to work on raising your self-esteem will be one of the key factors in whether or not you are able to move forward and successfully build the life of your dreams.

If you have low self-esteem, even if you've suffered with low self-esteem throughout your life, you can still develop strong healthy self-esteem by following through on the following 7 disciplines, each of which we will discuss in detail:

1. **Know and accept yourself:** this includes your strengths and your weaknesses.

2. **Recognise your innate value:** your valuable contribution to the world.

3. **Connect within daily:** through meditation and creation statements.

4. **Create a Personal Mission Statement:** identify what you will and will not tolerate and live by it.

5. **Own your creative energy:** by making choices with awareness.

6. **Prioritise your goals:** using your Wheel of Life.

7. **Be your own authority:** don't allow others to dissuade you or steer you off course.

By approaching your life in this manner from now on, you can achieve staggering results.

When I help clients build self-esteem, I often speed up the process by getting them to create self-empowered new declarations (Creation Statements) about who they are and what their valued contribution to the world is. Together with practising these declarations, they must also commit to embracing and embodying that inner value and then take the accompanying actions required to have it materialise in their own lives. Slowly, one step at a time, they begin to make the connection and experience themselves in a whole new way. This is a beautiful and humbling transformation to witness.

As you work on building core self-esteem, bear in mind that you have probably been living with self-deprecating habits for many years, or even decades. Be patient with the process.

Now, let's go through the steps for creating healthy self-esteem, one step at a time:

1. Know and accept yourself

Activating core self-esteem is largely about seeing the perfection in all that you are. This includes acknowledging your weaknesses as well as your strengths. You need to find the balance and learn to live in the centre of these two extremes, all the while appreciating the value and necessity of each extreme. If you think about it, we live in a world of duality – day and night, light and dark, good and evil, up and down - and the human psyche is no exception.

We all have strengths and weaknesses, the combination of which perfectly balance us as individuals, ensuring our essential contribution to life as a unique piece of the puzzle. We are not clones. We are designed to be different from one another, diverse in our individual expression of unique ideas, talents and preferences.

It's often not helpful when we label our strengths as "good" and our weaknesses as "bad". We then also label others in the same way, making unrealistic comparisons that cause us to judge them against our ideas of what is right and wrong. This is unfair because we are measuring them against our own personal beliefs, perceptions and ideals.

If we want to co-exist with others and have them appreciate and respect us for who we are, we must first find a way to fully appreciate and respect them for who they are as well. This will require that we give up those labels of "good" and "bad" because so-called "good" behaviours can tear down empires and "bad" behaviours can lead to miracles. All behaviours contribute to life, regardless of whether we are able to see the bigger picture or not.

Healing Action Step

Neutralising good and bad behaviours

Here is a simple exercise that will assist you in finding balance around what you perceive to be your own "good" and "bad" qualities which sometimes leave you feeling conflicted.

The purpose of this exercise is to show you that there are positives and negatives to all behaviours, even those we choose to label as "good" or "bad, or "strong" or "weak". If you do this exercise well you will really begin to appreciate how your "weak" or "bad" aspects serve you. You will also feel far more humble about your "strong" or "good" aspects.

a. List five behaviours that you feel proud to have as part of your makeup and then:

- For **each one**, go back through your memories and list

fifteen occasions on which engaging that particular behaviour had a **negative** impact on you and those around you. This is an important exercise so please dig deep until you find at least fifteen negative impacts for each of those five behaviours.

b. Now, list five behaviours that you feel inwardly ashamed of and then:

- For **each one**, go back through your memories and list **fifteen occasions** on which engaging that particular behaviour ultimately had a **positive** impact on you and those around you. Again, dig deep until the lights go on.

Life is grand and perfectly orchestrated. It is an eternal structure of perfect balance, even when we can't seem to experience this through our five senses. Every tragedy contains a blessing that will make itself known, in time. Equally, every blessing contains a tragedy that will too, eventually reveal itself. When you choose to label anything as "right" or "wrong", know that you're only looking at one side of something - half of the truth. Furthermore, when you label something as "right" or "wrong", you are choosing in that moment to accept or reject aspects of yourself.

Life is a mirror. Why is it that you like or dislike what you see? How could your "dislikes" serve you if you were to own them and how can your "likes" potentially harm you one way or another? It certainly is worth thinking about.

2. Recognise your innate value

In all my years as a practitioner in the healing and coaching profession, one thing I have repeatedly witnessed and have come to understand at a deep level is:

The speed at which you heal is directly proportionate to your level of self-esteem.

This may seem surprising to you but if you think about it, it makes a lot of sense and it applies to your physical as well as psychological healing. When you are coming from a mind-set that believes you are capable of overcoming anything, you attract the type of people, opportunities and circumstances that substantiate that. Things flow more smoothly and you move forward quickly with less resistance, healing at a more rapid pace. But when you come from a mind-set of loss and victimisation, you will equally attract people and events that bring more of this into your life. Those beliefs will keep you trapped, slow down your healing and can, in some instances, even bring it to a grinding halt!

Healing Action Step

Uncovering your innate value

In order to recognize your innate value as well as the valuable contribution you make to your world, let's go back to your Wheel of Life and complete the following exercise:

1. Using your journal, take out the list that you created in the final exercise of Chapter 3 (your empowerment audit). Rewrite the list, neatly, reversing the empowerment order so that the three areas **at the bottom** of your list (the areas in which you were least empowered) sit at the top of the list and the areas of higher empowerment sit at the bottom:

2. Starting at the top of your new list, and working your way

down, dig deep, identify and write down abilities you possess in each area that positively contribute to your life and the lives of others (you can use a fresh page for each area).

- Because the three areas at the top of your list are where you are least empowered, these are the areas that you'll need to focus on first and this may challenge you initially.

- I encourage you to keep looking and excavate your worth here! Look at what you have to offer the world and the people around you in that area. Look at how each of your inner qualities positively impacts other people in your life and how this helps power up their own Wheel of Life.

- Pay attention to physical abilities as well as mental/emotional intangible qualities - for example qualities like caring, nurturing, helping others become better in this area, etc.

3. Spend at least two hours on this exercise, going through each area one at a time.

4. When you are done, create a title on top of the first page that says "**I am valuable beyond measure because...**". Refer to this list often, with heartfelt appreciation for who you are and keep adding to the list when something new pops up that seems relevant.

3. Connect within daily

This part of building healthy self-esteem is established through setting aside time each day to engage in activities that enable you to expand your inner-connection. This will help you to stay in touch with your own thoughts and feelings and make decisions that are true to you.

As you should have your Essential Self-Care routine well established by now, here is a quick refresher of the daily activities that we have already identified for strengthening your inner-connection:

❀ meditation

❀ walking in nature

❀ deep breathing

❀ creation statements

❀ emotional and gratitude journaling

Connecting with your inner voice

With the advent of social media, the internet, game consoles and digital media, we live in a world where we are constantly bombarded with and over-stimulated by information, and we have lost the discipline of inner-connection. We are continually processing, filtering and reacting to millions of bytes of information that fly past our senses throughout the day and we are often barely aware of what we're feeling inside, particularly mute to the inner voice that's doing its best to guide us.

Even when we do hear this inner voice in our quieter moments, we often fail to act on it because we don't trust it. We doubt it, second guess it and seek approval on it. We procrastinate and run around in circles numbing ourselves with distractions, just in case, heaven forbid, we should hear a piece of guidance that asks us to give up something that lies within the confines of our comfort zone.

This is one of the reasons I included journaling, walking and deep breathing in the Essential Self-Care programme at the beginning of this book - it enables you to create a space in which to hear and feel yourself once more. It's also why I urged you to make it a life-long practice. Spending time with yourself in a relaxed and meditative state is an invaluable daily activity, essential for re-connecting back to the essence of who you are. It has a major impact on the quality of everything that you create because it allows you to build something magnificent with the help of your most insightful and valued guide – yourself!

Reflections:

Do you have a sense of your inner guiding voice?

How often do you follow through on this guidance?

If you would like to take things a step further, go back to the Wheel of Life exercise in Chapter 3 (where you created your vision for what you would like each area to look like in the future) and create a new affirmation, a couple of paragraphs long, incorporating your vision for each of these areas as though it has already happened.

When your affirmation is complete, read it every morning and night. Create a vision board (using pictures from magazines) that represent and embody what it is you are creating. This can be done as a collage onto an A4, A3 or any larger size piece of card, laminated and placed somewhere prominent where you can see it every day and really connect with the feeling behind each image, as if it has already happened.

Connecting with yourself in this way on a daily basis will bring much peace, love and self-appreciation into your life. In turn, you will extend this love and appreciation in service to others, perpetuating an exquisite cycle of grace.

4. Create a personal mission statement

Having your own personal mission statement is an essential ingredient in creating healthy self-esteem as it:

🌸 is a statement of clarity.

🌸 is a deep intention that paves the road ahead with clarity.

🌸 is a declaration to the universe about who you are and how you intend to claim all you desire.

🌸 defines your personal code of morals and ethics – that which you believe to be acceptable or unacceptable to you.

🌸 ensures that, when crossroads are reached and decisions need to be made, you will commit to choices that honour your true values above the instant gratification of the moment.

🌸 helps you resist the temptation to please or pacify others at your own expense, so ensuring that you never again experience the bitter taste of self-sacrifice.

As you move through your healing process, the two most crucial questions that you're now answering are:

1. Who am I?

2. Where am I headed next?

We've already addressed the second question in your Wheel of Life - now it's time to do some soul-searching around the first.

Knowing who you are and what you need to change in order to express it, is what your Personal Mission Statement is all about. It involves clarifying the following:

❀ The values and behaviours that are important to you, especially if you allowed them to be compromised in your relationship.

❀ What matters to you on both a local and international level. This includes the causes you support.

❀ Identifying the ways in which you know you need to change in order to breathe vitality into dormant aspects of your life.

❀ Behaviours that you value and what your deal-breakers are – things you absolutely will not tolerate from others from now on.

Let's move into the exercise of creating your Personal Mission Statement.

Healing Action Step

Your Personal Mission Statement

Your personal mission statement can be as simple or complex, long or short as you like. It can often take a couple of days, or even weeks, to refine so don't worry if you need to keep changing it. Once you begin to identify your core values, your awareness around your preferences will begin to expand and you will start to see things in a different way. This will instigate fresh new insights in the days and weeks that follow.

Your personal mission statement can include the types of future relationships you wish to attract, the kinds of people you do or don't want to associate with and the activities that you do or don't want to engage in. If it's important to you that your future partner is financially stable, or kind to your children, or supportive of your work and your beliefs, then include this is in your mission statement. Be clear about the top three to five things that really matter to you and factor them in.

Take a few minutes now to jot down thoughts that are already making themselves known regarding what to include. You may find it helpful to start your mission statement with "it is very important to me to..." (state desired qualifying criteria) and then follow with "I no longer tolerate..." (state criteria you wish to eliminate).

As an example, and with permission from Diane, a client who works as a health professional, here are excerpts of the mission statement she wrote once she had identified what she valued in her life. She carried this list with her wherever she went and never deviated from what she wrote in it. It guided her through some pretty tough decisions and helped her to construct a meaningful new life for herself.

• To recognise in each seemingly difficult situation, what it is I can and cannot influence and to take appropriate action and not dwell on my concerns and fears.

• To build engaging, meaningful, purposeful and lasting relationships in my professional and social life around the globe.

• To follow my intuition in relationships, and not subordinate to partner or peers.

• To know when to lead and when to follow, without being submissive.

• To regularly give to myself, not only the things that I so willingly give to others, but also the things that I wish others would give to me.

• To trust and honour my insight into every situation and build strength by taking responsibility for ALL of my decisions.

• To never indulge in gossip or allow others to complain to me about someone else without defending the absent party or showing those who are gossiping, another viewpoint.

• To always see or hear both sides before making a decision.

• To eat healthy food, take the appropriate supplements and rest well enough to be vital and alert each day in order to achieve my goals.

• To maintain my physical appearance, remain authentic to my own self-approval and love myself exactly as I am by affirming my appreciation for myself.

• To remember that stress leads to fearful thoughts and emotions – never to indulge in the instant gratification of making decisions from this place – especially in relationships.

• To save regularly and build financial independence. To master my income and not be a slave to budget spending. To apply the 24-hour rule of second thought before making non-essential purchases.

• To communicate and engage with others from a place of wisdom, compassion and authenticity without taking responsibility for their discomfort or humbling my response to compensate for their inadequacies.

- To stand proudly and confidently in the fullness of all that I have to offer the world.

- To spread joy wherever I go, showing appreciation for my family, my friends and my clients.

This example should give you a good basis for starting your own Personal Mission Statement. If you need a little more guidance, start by using your journal to create a list that resembles the following, using the same headings shown below:

Life Area	Who I am in this area	What I won't tolerate
Physical Well-Being		
Mental Treasure Chest		
Spiritual Connection		
Professional Path		
Financial Assets		
Intimate Relationships		

Social Network		
Personal Growth		

You should now be able to write your own Personal Mission Statement. When complete, put it up in your home somewhere you can see it clearly each time you pass by and carry a copy with you at all times as well so that you can read it as often as you need to.

5. Own your creative energy

Each one of us has access to a finite amount of energy every day. The amount that we can access largely depends on the lifestyle choices we make - the food we eat, how deeply we breathe, the amount of exercise we take, our sleep patterns and our energetic exchanges with others. It's a bit like an energetic bank account that gets topped up daily (more on this in the next chapter.) As we move through the day, we invest chunks of our energy into the different areas of our lives, directing it with our thoughts, emotions and physical activities - all of which require energy.

Each energetic investment we make yields a return. This return shows up as a match to the quality of the initial investment. What does that mean? It means that healthy choices (healthy thoughts and feelings directed towards ourselves and others) and healthy use of our energy (into physical activities) will yield good returns. However, negative feelings directed towards ourselves, others and circumstances – whether they are in the past, present or future - will not. Every person, object and event that we focus on is kept alive in our psyche's and, therefore, in our reality, trapping a portion of our energy along with it. And when you've used up your daily quota of energy, you will have no other choice but to take it from the only other available source – the cells of your body.

This is the reason why people who suddenly undergo intense stress soon begin to look as through they have aged ten years. Their physical bodies are being robbed of health and vitality through excessive anxiety. To counteract this, we must learn the mental discipline of preventing stress and anxiety from getting the better of us.

Most of us waste masses of our energy each day thinking about the past or worrying about the future. Is it any wonder that we sometimes feel so tired? Wasting precious life force by focusing on fear, jealousy, hatred, anger, guilt, remorse, worry or any other stress-inducing emotions, is something we really need to address if we want to free up creative energy in our lives.

Healing Action Step

How can I own my creative energy?

A great exercise for working with this is to notice what you're focused on and what you're thinking about as you go through your day and to STOP yourself mid-thought and make a different choice in that moment if necessary. Witness your limiting thoughts and introduce creation statements to re-direct your thinking. Whenever you find yourself worrying or obsessing about something STOP and ask yourself the following questions:

1. Will thinking these thoughts cause me to lose or gain peace of mind?

2. Is there anything I can do to alter this situation? If yes, what can I do? If no, this is out of my hands and I choose to let it go.

3. Will making this decision yield good energetic returns for me or place me further into energetic deficit? Does it reflect who I really am and who I want to become? What is the better decision to take?

Asking yourself these questions will allow you to take a step back and make a different choice. They will help discipline your mind and if you integrate them with your personal mission statement, the combination will help you build self-trust and self-esteem more effectively. Through this practise you will gain a deep insight into whether you make most of your decisions from a place of faith or from a place of fear.

6. Prioritise your goals

In order to effectively prioritise your goals you must learn to be *responsible* to, and not *for*. As women we very easily lose ourselves, taking on too much responsibility for our partners, children and friends. We often put their needs before our own, exhausting ourselves and complaining bitterly about the lack of appreciation and our own unmet expectations.

What we really need to learn is to be responsible to people but not for people.

Being responsible to someone means acting in a way that is wise and compassionate but also facilitates healthy communication about what your own needs, desires and limitations are in a way that enables the ideas and opinions of others to be considered, without negotiating yours away.

For example, you have set a goal to complete a particular study course, which requires that you factor in additional time each evening to accommodate the additional study. A dear friend, who loves to catch up every other night, pays no heed to the fact that you've told her you now have to study in addition to your usual responsibilities. She calls anyway and continues trying to keep you on the phone, seemingly oblivious to the subtle hints that you're dropping about not having enough time. You are responsible TO her by telling her calmly and directly that you will need to limit the amount of telephone conversations you can have with her in a given week. But you do not take responsibility FOR her reaction to this request. If she understands, that's wonderful - now you can both agree the evenings that work best. But if she reacts negatively - her reaction is not your responsibility, provided you have communicated clearly and compassionately.

Being responsible for someone means holding yourself accountable for tasks and responsibilities that someone else is perfectly capable of doing themselves. This is an extremely unhealthy dynamic, particularly if you're doing it with family members. Children who are old enough to be doing things for themselves, in no way benefit when you do it for them. Not only are you are robbing them of their own power and independence, you're robbing yourself of yours as well. This sets up co-dependent dynamics that can lead to the loss of self-esteem for all parties involved, encouraging subtle forms of manipulation, guilt trips and power struggles and I strongly urge you to discontinue this type of behaviour. You can only guide, teach or mentor someone else on what you have mastered for yourself. If your self-esteem is low, there is no way you can guide your children to healthy self-esteem. And you'll never build up your own self-esteem by taking it from someone else.

7. Be your own authority

Activating healthy self-esteem will require that you become your own authority. It requires that you take complete responsibility for yourself, your actions and your reactions. It demands that you develop a deep trust in yourself in addition to maintaining a profound connection with your own soul. Yes, you will have to confront the fear of making the odd mistake but is that such a bad thing? If you're always worrying about whether or not you're making the right decision, simply make the decision and decide to live or die by it, knowing that you can handle the outcome. Do this until you learn to trust yourself and your ability to make decisions.

Mistakes can sometimes be our best friends because they are nothing more than feedback systems, essential for growth. Anyone who has ever achieved anything in this world, including the great minds that have lived on this planet, only ever achieved greatness by trial and error. Thomas Edison made one hundred attempts at successfully creating the light bulb and this is exactly the way to approach life. We're more resilient than we give ourselves credit for and I hope you're starting to identify with that side of yourself. Believe in yourself, get comfortable with making mistakes and go for it! Trust in your ability to reach the ultimate goal. And don't you dare give up before you get there!

You may need a little practise in following your intuition and avoiding seeking approval from others, but being solely responsible for your decision-making will free up your creative energy and speed up your power to create. Don't get me wrong, the opinions of others can be really valuable at times but trusting your own intuitive hunches is far more important.

Healing Action Step

Becoming your own authority

Begin flexing your muscles of self-trust by setting the following challenge for yourself over the next 21 days:

• Pay attention to the decisions you need to make on a daily basis and notice how many times you feel the need to run a decision by a colleague, friend or family member before acting on it.

- Spend the next 21 days, practising the art of making EVERY personal decision you're faced with, completely on your own without running it by anybody, unless it requires specialised input (e.g. info required relating to legal matters, financial processes or any other specialised information that needs to be obtained).

You may find this exercise more challenging than you initially thought. Start with small decisions and gradually throw in some that are a little bigger as you go along. If a decision seems really overwhelming, allow yourself to sleep on it if possible. If you still feel unable to make it on your own, allow yourself to discuss it with one other person that you trust but remind yourself that you are only inviting in their opinion and you still need to make the final decision yourself.

Treat the decisions you make with reverence. Each one is contributing to the creation of your future and opening up potential doors. The smallest of decisions can have a major impact on your future.

Practise discernment, not judgement

Discernment is a healthy human trait as it helps us to follow our inner gut feeling about the people and circumstances we should engage with. It also allows us to know which activities are appropriate and which are inappropriate. It engages our intuition and can powerfully guide us to creating a joyous life. *Discernment says "I'm not judging - just noticing that this is or isn't right for me so I draw you closer or release you with love".*

Judgement and criticism on the other hand, can be more destructive traits that clearly reveal low self-esteem. When you judge someone else it's often because you are facing your own feelings of inadequacy, one way or another.

The old saying - that we do not see the world the way it is, we see it as we are – is so true. When someone behaves in a manner we find contrary, we often make all sorts of assumptions about why they are doing it based primarily on the reasons that WE would never behave that way. But none of us truly knows the whole story and all the contributing factors behind why people behave the way they do. We self-righteously dish out harsh judgement and criticism in a heartbeat. *Judgement and criticism says, "I don't like this or that about you because you make me feel uncomfortable, inadequate or small so I will stay away from you and tell others to do the same because I don't like the part of me that you represent and I refuse to look at it".*

Another wise teacher once told me that what you condemn, you become. It means that what you cause another to experience, you bring upon yourself to experience at some future point - so becoming the cause of your own effect. Ignorant perspectives always come full circle, returning to their creators as lessons for gaining new understanding. But we usually don't connect the dots. We call this karma. But do we stop hurting each other? No.

Judgement and criticism are absolute poisons to the quest of building an esteemed life and that especially includes judging yourself. If you judge and criticise yourself it won't be long before someone will show up in your life who is more than happy to judge and criticise you too.

Reflections:

How would your life change if you stopped judging yourself and instead acknowledged that you are doing the best you can?

How would your relationships with others change for the better if you were able to acknowledge them in the same non-judgemental way too?

A final word on choice and self-esteem...

A few years from now, I know some of you reading this book will write to me and share with me all the ways in which your lives and your relationships have become enriched. You will speak of the new friendships you've forged, the new careers you've embarked on and the new partners you've met. You'll describe the goals you are achieving and how happy and blessed you feel to be re-discovering yourself through empowered choice.

But some readers will have skimmed through this material, failing to put any of it into practice. In time, they will still feel sad, their hearts trapped in a hopeless vacuum, still all the while wishing that they could move forward but not quite able to shift their lives back on track. They will wonder what they are doing wrong and conclude that it's all down to fate or bad luck for them.

I wonder which of these two readers you will be. Right here! Right now! This is your point of power - the choice, as always, is yours.

It takes courage to establish the kind of boundaries that can effectively protect your dreams and all that really matters to you. That's where we're going next!

Chapter 7

Re-defining your
Personal Boundaries

"Comparing yourself to others only stunts your creative potential. Instead, follow your dreams for they are the hope of the future."

— Desiree Marie Leedo —

We have now determined the life you would love to create using your Wheel of Life and also established the importance of building an empowered core of true self-esteem from which to infuse and activate each area.

The third and final element that we need to establish is boundaries (both personal and inter-personal) as they are essential to protecting the things that you value most in life.

How Personal Boundaries Protect Your Wheel Of Life

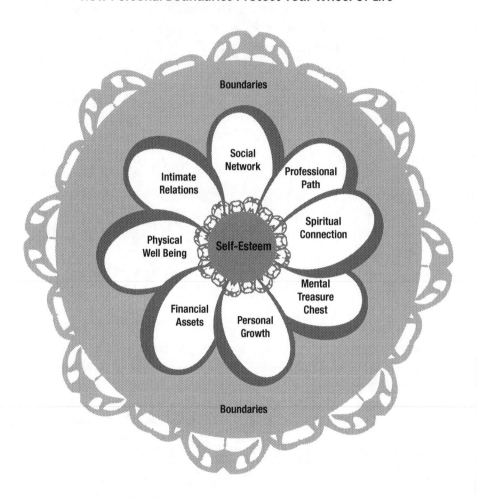

These **three cornerstones** will always enable you to build your strongest life - regardless of the people and events that move in and out of your space:

🌸 having a clear idea about the direction you want your life to take.

🌸 activating core self-esteem.

❀ establishing clear and distinct personal boundaries.

They will never fail you as the solid foundation on which your life can stand firm.

What are boundaries and why are they important?

Practising healthy inter-personal boundaries are as critical to the success of your life as the boundary walls of your home are in protecting your possessions from the outside world. Just like the walls of your home keep you and your possessions safe and contained, inter-personal boundaries allow you to safeguard your values, personal identity and the attainment of your dreams. In the same way that you would not allow outsiders to walk into your home and re-arrange the furniture or remove items without your permission, equally, you should not allow others to impose themselves on the more intangible, but still key, aspects of your life - like your time, your preferences and your goals.

Boundaries are essential because they are the only thing that clearly distinguish and differentiate you and your space from that of another.

Let's define those intangible aspects of your life that boundaries can help you to protect:

❀ your beliefs.

❀ your ideas.

❀ your goals.

❀ your vision for your future.

❀ your priorities as identified in your Wheel of Life.

❀ how you choose to prioritise the stuff that really matters to you.

❀ how much time you proportion to those who share your life.

❀ how much you invest into nurturing yourself and your own personal growth.

Establishing boundaries is important because it places a limit on the availability of your personal resources. It allows you to decide how much time, energy and attention you will invest into people and activities, but only once you have filled up your own cup first!

If you have ever heard yourself saying, "I can't believe (whoever) still expects more from me after everything I have already done for them" - that's a clear sign that there's a boundary issue at play somewhere.

When you feel victimised, disappointed or upset by the way someone is treating you, this is a clear indication that a boundary has not been clearly expressed. When we do not set and clearly express our boundaries, others will draw their own conclusions as to how much of our time and energy should be available to them, based on their own needs. In this way boundaries and expectations go hand-in-hand. It's up to us to take responsibility for what we can - and just as importantly cannot - commit to.

Rene's Story...

I'll never forget Rene, one of my first clients. She was one of the kindest, most loving and generous women I had ever met. She spent her life trying to be all things to all people and giving to others made her feel really good about herself. Rene could not recognize, at first, that her giving came from a place of needing to be liked and needed by others. There were clearly areas of her life (as well as things about herself) that she was quietly and desperately unhappy about.

One day, after attending a routine mammogram, everything suddenly changed for Rene. Her doctor informed her that she had a small cancerous lump in her left breast that required immediate surgery and a partial mastectomy. Rene, understandably upset, contacted close friends and family members to share the news. Soon afterwards, she was rather surprised when she discovered that they stopped contacting her. When she went in for surgery and asked some family members and close friends to help out with maintenance at home in her absence, she was shocked when they responded that they were just too busy to help out. It was painful watching this realization dawn on her - that even after everything she had given and all that she had done for these people, none of them were willing to inconvenience themselves and help out. After her surgery, only a couple of her friends came to visit and help her on the road to recovery.

It was a big wake up call that forced her to begin the painstaking task of sifting through who her real friends were.

At first she got angry, criticizing all those who she felt had let her down. But, in time, she found the grace within to view the entire event as an opportunity to identify those she could and could not truly rely on. She took ownership of the part of herself that was attracting the "needy" in her life and she saw how they had been feeding her own deep desire to feel needed. She realized that she had enabled every one of them with her self-destructive tendencies. She saw how she had been giving at her own expense and she took full responsibility for all the ways in which she had acted irresponsibly towards herself. It took a major health crisis to flag all this up.

Rene made a lot of changes after that. She took back her power, started fulfilling her own needs and learnt to value herself and her time again. She did not turn her back on her friends or family - instead she identified exactly what she was willing to do for each of them and she drew the line at that. She made more time for what mattered to her and was much happier for the experience. I am happy to report that her health has been perfectly fine ever since.

What weak boundaries will cost you

Having weak boundaries (or no boundaries at all) in place between yourself and others will ultimately result in the following disempowering experiences:

❀ Neglecting your own needs because you feel immense internal or external pressure from the demands placed upon you by others. This leads to resentment and bitterness at the expense of your own health and happiness.

❀ Experiencing an overall lack of vitality, depression or general disinterest in your own life because of the massive amounts of time and energy you pour into activities that you don't particularly like. You feel life is passing you by and that you're just existing, and not really living.

❀ You think, feel and speak like a victim because you feel powerless to change anything. This martyrdom approach destroys healthy relationships, costing you love and connections.

❀ You become addicted to the feeling of being needed each time you sacrifice yourself and you start doing things for others as a way to feel good about yourself. Dependencies are created, which costs all parties involved, their independence.

❀ In time, depression and personal identity crisis set in. You attract more and more people and events that over-step your boundaries. You fail to stand up or speak up for yourself, quietly resenting and criticising the seemingly fulfilled lives of others.

❀ Eventually, your body may externalise your internal cry for help by manifesting illness which forces you into make life-changing decisions so that you finally draw a boundary and claim back dying parts of yourself.

Women find setting boundaries particularly difficult. We often sell ourselves short a great deal in this area, because:

❀ We are natural nurturers and empathisers.

❀ We are sensitive to the needs of others, often less willing to prioritise and communicate our own needs.

❀ There is a subtle societal expectation that we should be the ones to make any required sacrifices.

❀ Once we become mothers we have an innate instinctual drive to put our families first, becoming all things to them, so ensuring that we nurture and protect the family unit.

Activating healthy boundaries means that YOU decide who you are and what's important to your life. But it's not about behaving in a ruthless, entitled or narcissistic way. You still need to behave responsibly and compassionately towards others, all the while ensuring that you are not affected by any guilt trips they may try to place on you. And yes, you may have to cut some people loose.

I have conversed with many phenomenally successful life achievers who all share the same truth: If you do not set the focus of your time and energy into activities that you consider a high priority, or if your boundaries don't align with what's most important to you, your life will swiftly fill up with low priority distractions. This is one of the most valuable lessons that I've learnt in my personal and professional life. If I wake up in the morning and invest time in planning and prioritising activities for the day, I will naturally honour those boundaries and make choices that ensure those priorities are met. I get everything on my list done and still have heaps of energy left at the end of the day. However, when I wake up thinking about what needs to be done as a priority but just "wing it", my day quickly fills up with one delaying distraction after another. I get very little done and by the end the day I feel tired, overwhelmed and frustrated.

Three Laws of Boundaries to help you stay in control

Don't fool yourself - when you start putting responsible boundaries in place, some of those closest to you, who are affected by them, may not respond well to the changes you are making. They may try to place all sorts of subtle and not so subtle guilt trips on you. That's because, at a deeper unconscious level, they don't want their personal dynamic with you to change. They are afraid that they may lose the ability to control you or get whatever it is that they are used to getting from their relationship with you.

For this reason, it's essential for you to understand the key principles behind establishing healthy boundaries so that you can fully re-claim your energy and your life.

The three principal laws that govern boundaries are:

- The Law of Conservation of Pain

- The Law of Responsibility

- The Law of Respect

The Law of Conservation of Pain

When two parties engage in conflict or a difference of opinion - the 'pain' ultimately ends up in someone's lap.

The person with the pain in their lap is the one who has not had their needs met in that situation, while the person who is offloading the pain **is** having their needs met and **is** controlling the situation.

If you practise poor boundaries - particularly if you have low self-esteem - it's pretty much a given that you're the one who generally ends up with the pain in your lap and that you feel pretty powerless in your ability to say NO when you should.

Some of the reasons you may find this so difficult to do, particularly in your more intimate relationships, are because:

🌸 you rely on others for security in some area of your Wheel of Life.

🌸 you need the approval of others and are afraid of being disliked.

🌸 you feel the need to be perceived as perfect and so try to be all things to all people.

🌸 you over-identify with others, taking too much responsibility for their general well-being.

🌸 you are afraid of conflict and try to keep the peace, even at your own expense.

🌸 you are afraid of being alone and don't want to face your dependencies.

It's not surprising to notice how many of these points relate to an underlying theme of low self-esteem.

Reflections:

Do any of the above themes resonate within you?

Are you usually the one who concedes when you engage in conflict?

Are you willing to take the necessary steps to change this?

When you begin to know yourself and what you are about, you can more easily break free of the suppressive dynamics of the Law of Conservation of Pain. While your Wheel of Life and Personal Mission Statement can assist you with this, you must also be able to break free of the fears you associate with setting healthy boundaries.

Healing Action Step

Setting healthy boundaries

Quite simply, this involves establishing your boundaries and delivering them in a way that ensures you get the outcome you need.

Refer back to your Personal Mission Statement and complete the following:

1. Choose an item that you wrote down as something you were no longer willing to accept or put up with. This could, for example, be time that you're investing or tasks that you're completing for someone who should be doing it for themselves.

2. Identify the person/people who are involved.

3. Write down the conversation you will have with this person/these people in which you will clearly, calmly, responsibly and compassionately state that you need to draw a boundary in this area so as to invest your energy into another area of your life.

4. As you prepare your "conversation", ensure that you first

communicate what it is you value about your relationship/ the situation with them. Then bring in the boundary that you need to set as well as the reason why you need to have it in place. Offer one or two solutions to the consequences of your having set this boundary but ensure that you leave the conversation without having compromised whatever it is that setting that boundary will achieve. Don't postpone the boundary or be roped into delay tactics, even if conflict arises. Refuse to let the pain fall into your lap.

4. Practise this conversation until you feel comfortable enough to have it for real. If it helps, use a mirror and, if necessary, practise calmly saying "no!".

5. Remember what we covered in the last chapter – be responsible TO and not FOR their reaction.

6. Release any guilt trips they may try to impose on you by writing down ten to twenty ways in which laying down this boundary will be beneficial to those you've just said no to.

The Law of Responsibility

You alone have sole responsibility for each and every aspect of your life.

While it can be tempting to include the opinions of others when making decisions, if you abdicate responsibility by allowing their opinions to over-ride yours, your life will never be your own. Instead it will be fragmented - with pieces assigned to all those who took decisions for you.

I'm not suggesting that there is no benefit to sharing problems or seeking advice. But when you are carving out a new direction it's vital that you are the one who is doing the directing. This means taking full ownership of each decision, how it will be implemented and where it will ultimately lead you.

Relying on the opinions of others can easily spiral out of control, creating an energetic loop that keeps all parties dependently tied to one another. Then, when one person disapproves, you can be sure that it will be easier to ditch your intuition than ditch the person concerned. Just don't do it.

Equally, you need to respect that others are solely responsible for their own lives too. Therefore, always encourage others to make decisions in line with what feels appropriate for them, regardless of what you think that may be.

Healing Action Step

Going solo on decision-making

Follow these seven steps to reclaiming confidence in your own decision-making ability:

1. Think of the person who you usually depend on for help when making decisions.

2. Reflect back on the results of decisions you took together that turned out to be in your worst interest, one way or another.

3. Ask yourself what the specific outcome was that you were afraid of, that prevented you from making that decision on your own?

4. Ask yourself what the other person is gaining by being involved in your decision-making process?

5. Identify how that person influencing your decisions is ultimately holding you back?

6. Spend the next week sleeping on each significant decision you need to make for at least one night and then see if you can make that decision yourself.

7. Complete the steps above with any other people that you regularly include in your personal decisions.

The law of responsibility requires that you stand behind a decision once you've made it. If the outcome is not to your taste, acknowledge that you have the creative power to make a new decision that will lead to a new result. You have the power to change anything - and that's the point! The power behind your decisions belongs to you and nobody else. You are responsible for the result of each of your decisions - whether you are making them for your self or allowing others to make them for you.

The Law of Respect

While we need to establish clear boundaries and have others hear and respect our NO, we must also be willing to hear and respect when others say NO to us!

Respect is a two-way street. Just as we expect others to hear and respect when we say NO to them, equally we need to be able to hear and respect when others say NO to us. While we may not always agree with the decisions or actions of others, becoming angry or resentful towards them for not wanting to do things your way is damaging and disempowering.

Trying to convince someone to change their decision to suit your agenda is even worse because it:

❀ Is an unhealthy form of manipulation that places pressure on another person to live according to your expectations.

❀ Weakens another person by causing them to doubt their own decision-making ability, thereby encouraging dependency on you.

❀ Draws you both into an unhealthy dynamic in which one person in the relationship exercises control over the other.

Reflections:

How do you respond to others when they say no to you?

Are you able to respect their point of view and make your decisions accordingly?

Or does this anger you, evoke rebellion or engage you in futile power struggles?

Effectively communicating your boundaries

The next crucial step is to communicate your boundaries both verbally and non-verbally in a way that ensures that they are heard and met with respect. Remember that the words you choose to speak, as well as the way in which you deliver them, will have a powerful impact on whether or not others will take you seriously because they ultimately convey to the who you are and what you will or won't accept.

Bear the following in mind when communicating your boundaries:

❀ How you deliver the message is as important as the message itself. Words that are aggressive and confrontational can evoke a confrontational response and do not communicate true power or authenticity. This includes the tone of your voice and the stance of your body. Your words should also never induce shame, humiliation or guilt.

❀ Phrases like "I don't know how…" or "I can't…" or "It's really hard to…" are viewed as defeatist and will most likely evoke an undesired response because nobody will take you seriously while you're not offering solutions. If you hear yourself speaking like this - stop! Instead, communicate your boundaries clearly while suggesting alternatives to those concerned in a way that enables your boundaries and also respects their needs. Use phrases like "I'm happy to…" or "I'm willing to do… which will enable us to…"

❀ Keep the conversation focused on the issue at hand and not on the person concerned. You do not want it to become personal as that can easily spiral into a larger or entirely new issue that becomes even more challenging to deal with.

❀ Your tone and body language should convey a calm certainty.

❀ Affirming the other person, the value you place on the relationship and the desired outcome are also important.

❀ Practise the art of hearing, respecting and accepting when others say no to you.

❀ Communicate your own "no" graciously, honestly and compassionately.

❀ If at all possible, communicate your boundaries in a way

that gives the other party a degree of choice. This introduces the possibility of win/win outcome and encourages mutual trust.

Reflections:

Is there a conversation you need to have with someone in your life around boundaries?

How can you best lead this conversation while holding the desired outcome in mind?

How can you best affirm the other person while delivering your message?

Healing Action Step

What does your body say about you?

Stand in front of a mirror and observe yourself. What does your body language say about you?

• Do you stand tall and confident? Or do you slouch at the shoulders giving off a self-defeatist impression?

• Do you hold your head up high and look others in the eye when you walk down the street or do you look down, trying to hide your face?

• Observe the expression on your face – is your face friendly and welcoming or do you scowl?

Now practice standing, sitting and moving around in a way that communicates confidence, openness and self-respect. Think of a boundary you want to put in place. Which facial expression or physical stance best supports your expression of that boundary? Notice this in the mirror. Use your Personal Mission Statement to help you with this exercise and ensure that your body language matches what you wish to communicate.

Does your body language betray your boundaries?

It's well documented that your body language accounts for over 80% of your inter-personal communication - whether words are exchanged or not. If you think about it, there's not much point in communicating a verbal message to others when your body language completely belies the words coming out of your mouth.

Body language should always re-enforce words that are spoken. It is also important to notice the body language of others. Notice those who project boundaries with confidence and those who do not, as well as how others react to each of them. Observing others is also a form of listening – a skill which is essential to effective communication.

Healing Action Step

Observe and practise!

1. Find a role model who practises great boundaries and observe their body language when they interact with others.

2. Construct the conversation you need to have with someone else about boundaries and practise it in the mirror, emulating elements of what you have observed through your role model until you are confident enough to have the conversation in person.

Don't get lost in translation

When you're setting boundaries, you're pretty much practising the art of saying no to something or someone in order to say yes to yourself. If you're someone who doesn't naturally handle confrontation well, you may need a little practice but that's fine. It's important to stick to the issue and not allow either party to get lost in the translation of what is *not* being said.

In a divorce situation, one of the first boundaries that will need to be established is between yourself and your ex. This doesn't occur to many people after they've broken up. They have gone their separate ways physically but mentally and emotionally they are still engaging their ex without having established suitable new boundaries, thereby exacerbating the challenges that exist around changing the behavioural dynamics towards each other, and so moving on.

Chrissie's story...

Chrissie's husband left her for another woman six years into their marriage and two years after the birth of their only child. When she ran through her divorce story with me, she spoke about it as if she was speaking about someone else. There were no tears. No emotion. Nothing but a half smile. She didn't want to move on and her ex kept coming back to the house for dinner and conversation. She cooked for him and continued to run his errands. She even attended one or two social work engagements with him, as if nothing had happened. Chrissie was clearly in denial! She didn't care who he had met or how he was treating her, in her mind she would do everything she could to hold onto the last fragments of their relationship.

Not surprisingly, Chrissie wasn't too interested in parts of my process, particularly those that assist in creating a new life. She left my office and said she would think things over. Three months later a very different and totally enraged Chrissie was back in my office. Yes, it took three months of subservience and passivity with her ex who was having his cake and eating it, for her to wake up and fully grasp that life as she had known it was over. He wasn't exactly choosing to leave the other woman and come back to the marriage. And when the rage started for Chrissie .... well let's just say that the old saying "hell hath no fury like a woman scorned" was fully embodied in her!

As we worked through the process, she courageously directed much of the anger she felt towards herself for being such a pushover, into the area of creating solid new boundaries. She changed the locks on the house and refused to communicate with him anywhere near the home where she needed to feel safe and develop her independence. She stopped taking his daily calls and only returned those that were relevant to legal proceedings. She found the courage to graciously inform him that she would no longer run any more of his errands and ignored all the messages he subsequently sent her, trying to make her feel guilty for her changed behaviour. The more boundaries she created to protect her new values, the less angry and the more calm and empowered she became.

When she was done, she channelled the rest of her energy into figuring out exactly what she wanted and going for it. By the time he was calling to say that he had made a mistake she was more than willing to agree with him and wish him well with the consequences of his choices.

Reflections:

Is there any part of Chrissie's story that you can relate to?

Where do you need to establish new boundaries in order to move forward?

How can you start putting those boundaries in place today?

Saying NO to self-doubt

In order to secure healthy inter-personal boundaries, you must break the habit of second-guessing and doubting yourself. Once you have set your mind on your goals, you need to remain focused on putting them into action and avoid getting tangled up in guilt. If someone attempts to place a guilt trip on you, the best thing to do is write a list of all the ways that setting boundaries with this person is going to be good for them - and then stop worrying about it!

It's essential that you learn to stand firm in your own authority, regardless of the actions and reactions of others, and be able to grant approval to yourself without self-destructing. You have already begun activating this process through the healing action step earlier about how to make decisions for yourself. Give yourself permission to do what it is you would love to do and stand firm if you sense that others are trying to manipulate you.

Be responsible TO others but not FOR others. If you consistently act graciously and compassionately you do not need to take responsibility for any undesirable response. You also do not need to perform tasks that they can complete for themselves. Break the cycle of dependency. Equally, break your own co-dependent relationship dynamics with others by avoiding asking them to complete tasks for you that you are perfectly capable of completing for yourself.

Always remember to practise the art of hearing, respecting and accepting when others say no to you. Once you have learned to say NO with respect, honesty, compassion and grace, it becomes a lot easier to set boundaries free of guilt.

Now it's time to take your final step and meet someone very special – the new emerging you!

Chapter 8

The New Emerging You

"Everything begins and ends with you - all else is simply reflection and deflection. You can choose to live a life of mediocrity or a life filled with meaning because you are the cause of your own effect."

— Desiree Marie Leedo —

I n this chapter we will integrate all that we have covered so far in this book so that you can pull it all together and begin to emerge an empowered life.

First, we will expand your awareness of personal power by looking at what it is and how to use it daily as part of your interactions with others. Then we will run through your energetic bank account and review the essential practice of how to bring what lies in your unconscious to your conscious awareness. We will revisit the Wheel of Life, illustrating how it can continuously be used as a lifelong tool for ensuring success. And finally, we'll examine how you can nurture your soul as you begin to emerge the new you.

Have you ever been in the company of someone with true presence? They may not even have uttered a word but you could feel the clarity, certainty, calm and influence they exude. When they speak they say what they mean and mean what they say without question. They are authentic.

I've used the term 'Personal Power' in other chapters and alluded to the fact that it is a profound magnetic radiance that emanates from calm, self-assured people who know exactly who they are and what they stand for.

Revisiting personal power

The word "power" has very negative connotations in our society, often conjuring up thoughts of dictatorship and oppression. This is NOT the kind of power I am referring to when I talk about personal power. On the contrary, personal power is active but gentle. It is fair and compassionate. It's not the type of authoritarian or aggressive power that comes from bullying power-hungry types who get their way by instilling fear, humiliation, manipulation or guilt in other people. I'm referring more to real, compassionate, calm, clear, fair and authentic power that radiates from people with influence. And you know it's real because others love to be around these people. They emanate a presence that often inspires others to their own greatness.

Nelson Mandela, Mother Theresa and Ghandi are all examples of people who radiate magnificent levels of personal power. At this time of writing, Mandela is still with us and continues to radiate great influence and integrity, despite the fragility of old age. Throughout their lives these people knew who they were and what they were working towards and they went about achieving profound results because they remained true to themselves and their purpose, directing their focus and their energies into people and activities who aligned with their purpose and their mission.

There are also many very normal people who emanate varying degrees of personal power, some of whom are successfully creating magnificent lives in which they serve humanity one way or another through their vision for a better world. But a better world always begins with you and an empowered person understands that. You cannot ever attempt to give of yourself when your inner point of reference comes from lack, fear or desperation. As Ghandi once said - you must be the change you want to see in the world - whether it's in your family, your community, your city or your country.

Reflections:

Think of someone you admire who acts from a place of personal power (it doesn't matter whether you know them personally or not).

Can you pinpoint the behaviours that person displays that you so much admire? Where in your own life do you see yourself as being able to display those same traits?

The secret to becoming a savvy and empowered woman

It is my hope to be able to empower you to the point where you know that, no matter what's headed your way in the future, you have all the necessary tools and know-how to bring yourself through it effectively. To have you know that you can handle any situation and to feel that you can live your life as a confident and independent woman from now on.

So, how do we expand our own personal power? Is personal power something we either were born with or we weren't? In fact, while it may come naturally to some, for those to whom it doesn't, it certainly can be developed with sincere commitment. Personal power is nothing more than a deep, esteemed and clear inner acknowledgement and acceptance of who you are, where you are headed and what you stand for combined with an ability to express yourself in a way that is gracious and compassionate to others, while making choices that are true to who you are.

Every step we have taken throughout this book so far has been a step towards helping you develop your own personal power.

We have already:

❀ Identified what it is you want through your Wheel of Life.

❀ Identified what you will and won't stand for through your Personal Mission Statement.

❀ Started developing your self-esteem and established effective boundaries.

You already have these aspects all worked out. Now all we need to do is apply the glue that holds them all together - Choice and Will!

It's one thing to know who you are, what you stand for and where you are headed. And it's another to be able to apply self-esteem and personal boundaries. But these are all still merely fragments that need to be glued together in order to create and express the collage we call personal power. None of the above fragments will stick if you cannot courageously apply strength of **will** to each of your **choices**.

This step is key! In order to create the life of your dreams, you are going to need to need to be mindful of *how* you apply *choice* and *will* to every decision you encounter and you are going to need to communicate with respect and honesty because each choice you make will either take you one step closer or one step further from what it is you desire.

Without the courage to make choices that align with who you say you are and what you say you want, none of what you are working towards will ever truly transpire – you must make decisions in a way that honours the priorities you've chosen through your Wheel of Life and Personal Mission Statement. If all of these elements do not line up, success will never be attained.

So, how then do we start to emanate personal power and become that savvy empowered woman? Quite simply, through the consistent application of:

- **Choice** – consistently engaging your power of choice in a self-responsible way.

- **Will** – activating the courage to make choices that will materialise your goals.

Reflections:

Have you ever taken a moment to reflect on where some of your choices may lead you?

Do you tend to make choices on "auto-pilot" without giving much thought to whether they are empowering or disempowering?

How can you begin treating the choices you make with more reverence?

Behaving authentically plays a huge role in becoming an empowered person. That's because authentic people know how to express themselves and their preferences both verbally and non-verbally.

People who behave authentically:

- Are true to their personal beliefs and values and can deliver tough messages in a compassionate way that does not intimidate others.

- Know how to keep themselves separate when appropriate.

❀ Know how to behave responsibly towards others without taking responsibility for them.

Know their limitations and don't make promises they cannot keep. They know they are only as good as their word and people respect them because they respect themselves.

Reflections:

Do you identify with the statements above?

How are you already displaying a great sense of authenticity in your life?

Are there any areas that you feel you may need to develop?

Your energetic bank account

If we look at personal power from an energetic point of view, it's easy to see how people with personal power understand the mechanics of how to distribute their life force effectively. They know how to make wise energetic investments that harvest healthy returns. They also know how to refrain from pouring energy into "bottomless pits"- people and situations that drain them and deliver zero returns, causing them stress and anxiety instead and leading them into an energetic deficit.

So what does this look like in our day-to-day lives? What is an "energetic investment" and how are we engaging in all of this consciously or unconsciously every day?

We touched on our energy quota in the previous chapter – the amount of energy we have access to daily and how we spend it. Now we will go into this in a little more detail as it's particularly relevant to building personal power.

Each of us has an energetic bank account (a daily quota of energy available to us based on the quality of the lifestyle we lead). We access this energy through the quality of food and water we consume, the exercise we take, the air we breathe and the amount of sleep we get at night. This daily influx of energy is the equivalent of our **energetic income**.

Energy taken in is then converted and *stored* in the cells of our bodies, ready for release to assist with:

❀ fighting disease.

❀ growth and repair within the body.

❀ physical energy required by the muscles.

❀ balance of internal metabolic and hormonal processes.

❀ energy required for mental and emotional processes.

This stored energy is the equivalent of your **energetic savings account** and the energy it takes to perform each of the above constitute your **energetic withdrawals**.

If you're someone who over-thinks things, worries a lot and stresses easily with no outlet for that stress - chances are you feel pretty exhausted. When you live in the past or worry about the future, you lose energy to the objects of those thoughts and emotions. Where the thought goes, the energy flows.

If I could show you this in energy terms, you would literally see streams of energy leaving your body in all directions with every thought you think and every emotion you feel. If the thought and emotion is positive and healthy, it builds grace and returns more energy to you. But when it's negative or hurtful, it attracts more of the same and you become consumed with negative thought and emotion. Your system has no option now but to take the extra energy you're pouring into those stressful encounters from the only other place that it's available – the cells of your body. Now, you're in **energetic deficit** and your personal power is quickly depleted.

When you choose to flow with life, surrender your anxieties to a higher power, free up your mental and emotional energy by staying present and invest your energy predominantly into thoughts and emotions that contain seeds of grace, you yield high energetic returns and your energy soars.

What I have found interesting in my years as a practitioner, is that the way a person handles their energetic bank account is often reflected in the way they handle their actual bank account. It may sound crazy but I have seen, time and time again, that a person's ability to manage their relationships, manage stress, feel empowered and enjoy success in their lives (finances included) is strongly linked to how they manage their energy. It's like a thread that runs through every area of their lives and it's intimately linked to their sense of self-worth, their personal boundaries and the choices they make.

Making the unconscious conscious

If you've been completing the exercises in this book and digging deep, I know you have come a long way in making much of what lies deep in your unconscious, conscious. Well done! Did you know that this is the key to releasing negative behaviours that you are holding onto deep down inside? As you may have discovered, this isn't always easy but it does deliver results.

The best way to let go of limiting unconscious beliefs and behaviours, is by shining the light of awareness on it. This means becoming aware of what stands in the way of you living your full potential in this world. After all, that's what the journey of life is all about.

How do you do this? By asking the right questions – the kind of questions you have been asking throughout this book. As the new you continues to emerge, you'll find you need to make a choice - to live with full awareness, or half-awareness.

Living with full awareness will lead to your taking ownership for the entire spectrum of your life. Living with half awareness will lead to your only taking partial ownership of your life - thereby producing partial results. This means that any aspect of your life that you have not taken ownership of will continue to control and direct you from the outside. Subsequently, you will feel that you have no control. You will then dismiss your creative power and conclude that the aspects that aren't manifesting are down to fate.

While we certainly can't spend our lives analysing every person and event, it is useful to notice when we get angry, upset, resentful or afraid. These are red flags to some inner resistance that we need to address in order to move forward. There is an entire world full of people and events out there that are helping us everyday to make the unconscious, conscious.

Reflections:

Have you decided whether you are ready to take FULL ownership for every aspect of your life?

Are you willing to do what it takes to be the sole director of the movie of your life?

Healing Action Step

The power of why, what and where

The three words to introduce when you're working to make the unconscious, conscious are: WHY, WHAT and WHERE. Here are some examples for how they can be applied:

1. WHY am I angry with this person? WHAT button are they pushing inside me? WHERE does that come from?

2. WHY can't I tell (whoever) how I feel? WHAT am I afraid of? WHERE am I afraid the situation will end up?

3. WHY do I feel so jealous? WHAT happened in the past that caused me to feel this way? WHERE will my future relationships end up if I don't work this out for myself?

You can use the words WHY, WHAT and WHERE in a variety of combinations and re-apply the same question repeatedly if it helps. Sometimes you have to ask the question five layers deep (meaning that you apply the words at least five times to the same dilemma) in order to get to the unconscious fear or belief. Keep these words close to hand and apply them whenever you feel upset – it's a powerful way to deal with all your red flags.

Letting go of pain

Once you have made the unconscious conscious, how you do you let go of the pain? You **decide** to let it go. I'm sorry if the answer sounds too simplistic but it's the only answer there is. Exactly in the same way as you would decide to let go of a scalding pot once you have picked it up and realised it's burning your hand.

Do you remember the exercise we did in Chapter 5 in the section "Feel the Fear" where we focused on feeling the fear intensely in a relaxed state and continually inviting the feeling back until it dissipated? You can apply that same exercise here when you are working to release something painful. Alternatively, you can simply decide that you are done with it and let it go! It really can be as simple as that.

I had a client a few years ago who profoundly exemplified this approach in her healing journey!

Linda's story...

Linda was a bright and cheerful woman who adored her family and worked part-time at a solicitor firm. She was one of those people that would brighten up a room with her infectious smile and her positive approach to life and people loved being in her company. When her husband of seventeen years left her for his secretary a couple of months after her mother had passed away, Linda recoiled, overnight, and became one of the most pale and withdrawn women I had ever seen. My heart practically broke as I sat listening to her story, watching her struggle not to fall apart as she tried to animate the very last fragments of remaining strength in the face of her deep hurt and sadness.

I knew that Linda was one of those women who, once she had worked through her process, would use this experience to create something positive in life. And she did indeed immerse herself in her healing process, though largely to distract herself from the pain she felt. But as she diligently followed her essential self-care programme she started enjoying the benefits of eating healthily, exercising and spending quality time in her own company, something she hadn't done in years. She was committed to figuring out who she was and what she wanted from the rest of her life. She knew she was at a crossroads and could now choose a life of mediocrity or a life filled with meaning.

Linda realised that she actively needed to let go of the feelings of betrayal that she was holding onto for all she was worth. These were simply her last ditch attempts to exercise control over the situation and her soon to be ex-husband. She came to recognise that she had acted with integrity throughout her marriage and that the consequences of her husband's actions were not hers to bear. She also realised that just because her husband had betrayed her, that didn't make her a bad person. More than that, she came to accept that he was not a bad person either. In the moment that she realised she truly had nothing to regret, she was able to let go and embrace her freedom.

Through healthy eating and daily exercise, she began to shed the excess weight that she'd gradually picked up over the years and her renewed vitality spurred her on even further. She re-connected with herself on a deep level and chose to "lock down her day" (step ten) by keeping her "support angels" – some personally meaningful talismans, given to her by special people throughout her life. She gained strength and support from them and carried them in her pocket wherever she went. As she had not yet entirely come to terms with the loss of her mother she also carried a locket given to her by her mother shortly before her passing. She would proudly produce all these items from her pocket and tell me how much love and strength she gained, simply by holding them whenever she felt she was falling apart.

She began to share all her feelings and gratitude's in her journal as if she was speaking with her mother, so re-establishing a connection with her, enabling her to heal from that great loss. She also loved using creation statements, replacing each one with a more powerful version as soon as it "felt complete" for her.

Linda transformed remarkably quickly for a woman in her situation and it was stunning to witness how she reached out and healed the lives of so many other women in the process. She was someone who truly understood the meaning of supporting others in what it is you most want for yourself. Amongst other new ventures, she started a small divorce group in her area. It began as an informal gathering for women who were in a similar situation as a way to support each other by sharing their own journeys. She invited other inspiring women from all walks of life to come and speak to her group and her venture grew from strength to strength. It wasn't long before she gained recognition in her community for her work in setting up a highly valued and successful group for women going through divorce.

Linda will achieve great things in life – not only because she is driven to serve others, but also because she has gained authentic connection to her own personal power. She lives a meaningful life in which, despite the challenges she may have faced throughout the day, she feels deeply fulfilled every night when she goes to bed and she knows that she can make change anytime she likes because she sees herself as the beginning and the end of her own experience.

The Wheel of Life – Your Constant Companion

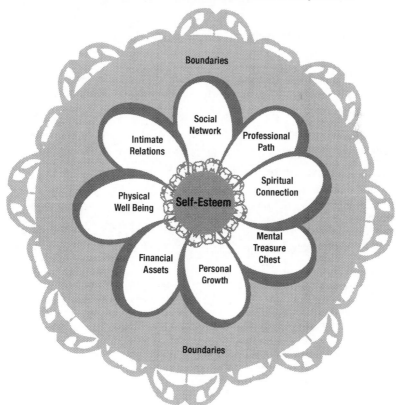

While the circumstances of your life will forever be changing, knowing who you are and what you want in every area of your life will always give you a strong connection to yourself and your future. The key to appreciating and enjoying your life is to have fun, to love and to laugh from a *place of wholeness*. And to choose your partner, job, friends and activities, not from a place of dependency or desperation, but *from a place of wholeness*.

Keep challenging yourself to grow - make your Wheel of Life your greatest friend. Ensure that it is an integral part of your life from now on. There are so many ways in which you can work through countless issues using this amazing wheel.

Healing Action Step

Continually refining your life goals

As you continue along your path of creating a self-fulfilled life, you will need to revisit your goals every six to twelve months in order to ensure that your goals are realistic and that you are making lasting progress, so staying on track. You can then make any necessary adjustments to your original goals or re-focus any area you choose, as follows:

1. Refer back to the Wheel of Life that you completed in Chapter 3, isolating the areas that you perceive as a priority (usually what is lowest on your empowerment audit list).

2. Take one of the goals that you wanted to achieve in that area and write down five action steps that you can take immediately towards achieving that goal.

3. When you are done, take the next goal in that area and write down five action steps that you can take today to-

wards achieving that goal too. Continue to work through that entire area until you have chunked each goal down into five action steps. If the goal still seems too overwhelming or too big to achieve then chunk each of those five action steps down even further - until you have identified enough distinct action steps that you are easily able to see all the steps required to make that goal a reality.

4. Once you have achieved your goals in that area, set new goals and move on to the next area that is low on your list of empowerment. Approach that area in the same way.

5. Ensure that you at least tackle the bottom three areas on your empowerment list, in other words the three areas in which you are least empowered. Once you start to turn these areas around you will feel amazing and you can then focus on further strengthening the areas at the top of your list, if you so choose.

6. Once this list is complete and you have all your action steps in place, use your diary and schedule times and dates against each of these action steps. Then stick to them!

7. As you begin to achieve your goals, reward yourself along the way! And more importantly - *set new and bigger goals!*

Feed your soul and catch the magic moments

Now we come to one of the most beautiful practice of all – that of feeding your soul. On my own spiritual path I've become very aware of the "being" versus "doing" way of living ife.

"Being" is the state of simply being, without resistance, and allowing life to flow. "Doing" is a state of taking action in order to instigate change in a certain direction. Many spiritual disciplines advocate "being" as the ultimate state of enlightenment while many high achievers will opt for "doing" as the only way to push, push, push life forward.

I'm a greater believer that the truth is always in the middle which is why many of my methods encourage both "being" and "doing" in balance. It's important to be able to identify the changes you want to make and have the ability to take action, but it's equally important to know what nourishes your soul and allow yourself to nurture that each day.

It's the balance of "being" and "doing" that will always deliver the most meaningful, self-fulfilled life. Without matter, spirit is expressionless. Without spirit, matter is motionless.

Healing Action Step

How to feed your soul

- Make a list of at least ten things that feed your soul. It could be the sound of your breath during meditation or enjoying a piece of classical music. It could be walking in nature, a hug from your children or your pet or a sunset walk along a beach. It could be reading an uplifting piece of literature or a solitary bubble bath by candlelight to soft background music.

- Starting today, incorporate at least one of these activities into your day – *every day.*

- Practise mindful and heartfelt appreciation when you engage in this activity as this should not be a mechanical exercise.

> • Allow the sensations of connection and well-being to flow through your being. Allow the pleasure of the moment to fill you up and nourish your soul.

The journey back to self-love

The journey of your life is a journey to love. Love is a powerful and, often, misunderstood force. It cannot be theorised, only felt in the rare moments that we feel true connection and acceptance for all that exists, as it is, in that moment. Contrary to popular belief, it is not the emotion of infatuation or adoration that we feel for a new lover – instead, it is a steady connection to the present moment. It is not conditional, but all encompassing.

What keeps us from experiencing love in each moment? Quite simply, it's our layers and layers of resistance to the acceptance of the present moment, exactly as it is, and without judgement. It is near impossible for the majority of us to be present in a state of love as we move about our lives with so much fear, anxiety and anger at play. These emotions are nothing but pure resistance and we escape them whenever we can by distracting ourselves with one "feel good" activity after the next, in order to obtain a little relief wherever we can. When trauma strikes, however, it becomes impossible to escape the layers of pain stuffed down in our unconscious and, as it all surfaces with great intensity, we become entangled in the web of our own resistance, unable to break the illusion and see past our pain.

Rachel's story

Rachel discovered a powerful way to activate her own healing process when she realised, during a consultation, that no two emotions can occupy the same space at the same time. For her, that was a revelation. She noticed that when she stopped to appreciate the beauty of a flower or a sunrise, she

was momentarily completely removed from her pain. She also noticed that when she went out of her way to help someone in a self-responsible way, she was less focused on her own heartache than she was on the care of her fellow human being.

Although she never abdicated responsibility for any step in her healing process, she healed so much faster simply by expanding the practise of stopping and "being present" with the intricate beauty of a flower, enjoying the slow crashing sound of waves on a beach or becoming fully present, almost one, with the flicker of a flame. Through nourishing her soul she came to realise that she had not "lost love" after all.

She came to see that her "loving feelings" for her ex were in fact only an activation by him of the vast well of love already contained within her, and that this love was all still hers to access whenever she liked! Without even realising it at first, Rachel was allowing her presence with the beauty of nature to open up the love in her heart in the same way as her ex had done. Her path to self-love and healing was one of the most beautiful things I have ever witnessed and I will always remember her as an amazing soul.

The New Emerging You

This book has demanded that you heal yourself physically, emotionally and psychologically. It's demanded that you identify and face some of your biggest fears and challenges. It's encouraged you to connect with yourself at a very deep level and take ownership of every aspect of your inner and outer life. And as you've worked through the chapters and exercises, little by little, the new you has slowly begun to emerge.

Every step in this process has been designed to move you closer to a state of love because it is only when you release your inner resistance that the new you can emerge fully. And when you can connect with who you are at this deep level from a place of real self-acceptance and self-love, only then will you truly be capable of loving another.

You now have all the keys you could ever need to unlock the doors to a beautiful and bright future. All you have to do is put them into practice. This is the time for the new you to emerge in all its glory. You are a goddess! You are a woman who holds the power to envision, create and birth new life. Your innate gifts of warmth, sensitivity and nurturing bestow the true power upon you of what it is to be a woman.

There's only one more piece of the puzzle left uncovered. I'm sure you can guess where we are headed next...

Chapter 9

Finding Love Again

"The journey of life is a journey to love with every encounter gently urging you to awaken to love instead of falling into a deeper state of despair."

— Desiree Marie Leedo —

A s you move through your healing process and begin to emerge your new life, at some point love will love will find you again through someone new. Many women want to know how long after their divorce, or breakup, they should wait before looking to start their next relationship. My answer is this – as long as it takes for you to attain real emotional balance and a good degree of inner and outer independence.

How will you know when you have attained this? Quite simply, you will know it innately. Certainly, nobody else can tell you this. You will feel the time is right to start anew and you will feel empowered enough to want to make change.

The journey to new Love

It's common for women who have been through a divorce to have a series of "mini-relationships" before they meet the next person they settle down with. This is often because they are unconsciously afraid and need to "test the waters" before committing again. The principle that we previously covered relating to "the outer reflecting the inner" is particularly key to bear in mind when you feel ready to start loving again. If you are still coming from a place of low self-esteem, lack of personal boundaries, lack of direction or self-doubt, chances are you will attract a relationship that directly reflects that back to you.

Debbie's story

Debbie was a client who was committed to making a full inner and outer recovery after an exceptionally turbulent emotional ordeal brought on by the breakup of her marriage. She decided to have male friends that she could meet for coffee or dinner but she refused to become involved with anyone until she had completely taken back the reigns of her life. When she did start dating again, she attracted two short relationships in quick succession, both involving men with commitment issues. When she came to see me feeling distressed about whether or not to persevere, we looked at how she was really feeling inside about committing to a new relationship. She soon realised that she was still feeling afraid to fully commit for fear of being hurt.

By looking at the dynamic between her and the men she had been attracting, we quickly pinpointed a few unresolved issues around self-esteem. Debbie saw exactly why she had attracted these men and we worked through the remainder of her fears in two short sessions. Her next relationship lasted six months and, although she really liked the man she was seeing, she did not feel a close connection and he wasn't always treating her with the kind of respect she knew she deserved. She recognised that when she had first entered into the relationship she was still lacking self-confidence in expressing herself as the new woman she was in the process of becoming. She decided to break it off and worked through the last of her inner obstacles. Five months later she met a wonderful, kind and loving man, and a year and a half later they were walking down the aisle.

Before You leap

Until you have moved through your healing process in its entirety and can feel yourself emerging from the dark tunnel and into the light with an open heart, I do not encourage becoming involved in a new romantic relationship. This is because every new relationship starts with inherent foundations and intentions - if these are not based on wholeness and integrity, the relationship is unlikely to go the distance.

Before getting involved again, be sure that you have at least spent enough quality time in your own company and become fully re-acquainted with yourself. Take the time to rediscover and pursue interests that reflect who you are as an individual - interests that you may have given up on while you were in your prior relationship, as well as any new interests that you may wish to develop. Enjoy the company of new people you meet along the way. Have fun and arrange to meet others socially. **And most importantly, become the type of person you would like to meet.**

As you start to engage life as a fully integrated individual with your own set of interests, you will begin to love your life again and become irresistible to those around you.

New relationships - what to avoid

When embarking on a new relationship it's important to be able to discern which issues belong to you and which belong to the other person. If you find yourself continually coming from a place of fear and insecurity then it's your responsibility to commit to addressing and healing those issues within yourself. However, if you are genuinely not being treated with respect then it's not the relationship for you!

This is why it's so important to enter a new relationship from a place of wholeness. If you have low self-esteem, poor boundaries and no sense of direction, you are easy prey to attracting a domineering partner and a life of submission and manipulation.

Essentially you should always maintain complete ownership of at least fifty percent of each area of your Wheel of Life so that your new relationship does not start from, or slip back into, a place of dependence or powerlessness.

Here are some classic signs of unhealthy behaviour to avoid when embarking on new relationships. Repeated displays of any of these behaviours are a red flag and should cause you to question whether the relationship is really right for you.

- Showing blatant disrespect towards your ideas, family, social circles, ambitions, values, what you stand for, etc.

- Mental or emotional manipulation that prevents you from pursuing your own interests or alters your behaviour to make them feel more comfortable or secure.

- Making you feel guilty for wanting your own needs met.

- Expecting that you make the majority of sacrifices and fit in with his schedule.

- Loss of temper, shouting, any signs of violence, etc.

- Repeatedly being dishonest - no matter how big or small.

- Playing control games – keeping you in the dark, not responding to you at times or withdrawing when it suits him.

When true love comes knocking

When you do find new love and you know that it's right, it's a wonderful thing. There is much to be said for the way in which real love truly does conquer all.

Many women also mistakenly think that it's possible to be one hundred percent healed before becoming committed again. As much as we can go most of the way towards this, the truth is, it's not entirely possible for those who have been badly scarred. Just as you would go to University or College, get an education and not actually be able to apply it until you are immersed in the experience of the job, so it is not always entirely possible to complete your healing in its entirety until you are immersed in your next committed relationship. You can definitely get yourself almost all the way there on your own (by working through your issues as we've been doing throughout this book) but that last small percentage will usually occur through the love of the person who is destined to stand by your side and share the rest of your journey through life. This is how you know that it's real.

In your new relationship, it's quite possible that some of your hurts and insecurities will re-surface as you start to give your heart and your trust to someone else again. This can also be one of the pivotal ways to recognize whether this person is the right person for you or not. If you have been responsible in your own healing process and resolved your own issues, fears and self-doubt, I believe that the right person will walk you through this final step. Within reason, any new relationship that does not show this type of potential and puts you under any sort of pressure needs to be re-examined. Go slowly and gently - this is the rest of your life we're talking about and you deserve the very best.

My own story...

On my own journey along the seemingly endless road back to love, I probably made every mistake there is to make - from playing the victim, to doubting myself, to wanting desperately to pull the covers over my head and wait for someone to rescue me. I dated the wrong people but learnt so many things about myself.

Through the grace contained within a twisted experience, I had an epiphany one day. I realised that nobody was coming to rescue me and that I was one hundred percent accountable for who I was and who I was becoming. And worse, I realised that if I didn't take control I would slide so far down that I wouldn't be able to get back up again. That was the day I woke up and started paying attention. It was the day of reconnection and to this end I thank every difficult encounter I had along the way, because that day real hope was re-ignited deep inside me.

So, this time, when one of my very dear girlfriends called to whine about how there just aren't any good men out there anymore, I responded quite differently. I told her that I no longer believed that to be true - that I believed we were creating our own experience and that it was the combination of what we kept expecting to show up as well as the vibes we were putting out because of our own unresolved issues, that were leading us to think this way. She didn't sound convinced but I clung to my new revelation and kept affirming that there are plenty of good men out there and that, when the time was right, I would find the perfect one for me.

And then I worked at becoming the kind of person I wanted to date. The more time I spent being kind to myself, developing my interests, expanding my social circle and enjoying time in my own company, the more I started to appreciate myself. By the time I reached the point of being completely self-sufficient and self-appreciative, I no longer wanted to be in a relationship! I was having that much fun.

Not long after that, just around the time my friend was calling me up yet again to complain about the lack of good men in the world, I met my partner, out of the blue and in the last place I would ever have expected. He was everything I could have hoped for, and more.

Even though, at first, I still had some minor trust issues relating to my past, he was never impatient or irritable. He held my hand, supported me with open and honest communication and ensured that his life and everyone who shared it were totally transparent. We had both came to the relationship open about who we were and where we had come from without any expectations that either of us was perfect, and committed to the life that we wanted to build and share together. The deep trust that developed between us also provided a space for him to iron out his own minor issues, with my loving support. Now we are committed to building a beautiful future together. I have returned to the heart of love and when I think about the road ahead, I do so knowing that I have never felt more complete, both as an individual and as a partner.

You are more than just your mind

You need never accept the reality that you see before you as absolute. What you see in your world today is here because of your best beliefs, thoughts and creations of yesterday. Today is your point of power. Today you can make a different choice and create a different tomorrow, whichever way you want it to be. You now know exactly how to do just that. Yes, it will take some work, some time and a lot of effort but nothing in life that's worth anything will come to you any other way. And the gifts you will gain along the journey will make it all beyond worthwhile.

Don't identify with your mind because it's not the truth of who you are. It's merely a tool for reasoning and rationalizing. You are not your thoughts – you are the pure and beautiful being that is having your thoughts and those thoughts can always be changed. Connect with your soul, your essence and discover the truth of who you really are. You are not your past or your future. You are timeless present moment awareness.

I challenge you to find the "you" from the past or the "you" in the future. You will never find them because you are always the consciousness that exists in this moment - the rest is purely memory or imagination, fear or anticipation. Identifying with your mind keeps you locked into the reality of time and space - you are so much more than this! You have fragments of stardust sitting right there in your DNA and you are connected, through your molecular structure, to the entire universe! How awesome is that? No need to play small then. No need to remain trapped in the illusions of time and space.

The past no longer exists and the future never actually arrives. All that you have is this moment. Right now. This is the moment on which you build the next moment – this is your point of power for re-arranging the atoms of the universe into the glorious manifestation of your future creations.

Coming full circle...

A nd so we have come full circle. Today, the young woman at the beginning of our story who had her heart so devastatingly broken, lives in gratitude for the sweet nectar unleashed by the splinters of her experiences.

When she looks in the mirror today, she smiles knowingly to herself in full acknowledgement of the beautiful life that she has created. She likes herself and has come to love the way in which her warmth and sincerity touch the lives of others, inspiring them to their own greatness.

She has come to embrace her weaknesses in full appreciation of how they keep her humble and grounded and how they profoundly contribute to the whole and perfect being that she is. She has learnt the difference between the quality of experiences created from a state of self-connection and those created from a place of disconnection.

She has accepted the hand of friendship, extended to her by her former husband, and she lives in utmost respect of the sincere and caring friendship they have forged, along with the many ways in which he continues his support of her.

She has taken the reigns of both the masculine and feminine energies within, knowing when to lead and when to follow without being submissive. She stands as firm in her courage as she does in her compassion and she understands that to become a leader, one must be just as comfortable with being unpopular as one is with being popular.

She has come to recognise her inner goddess and the more she matures, the more she thrives on the vast depths of love and wisdom that lie deep within her soul. She understands that radiating inner beauty is like a priceless jewel, always able to bestow freedom from the superficial shackles of modern society.

She spends less time self-deprecating and more time self-accepting. She looks to the future, thinks to the future and creates for the future, all the while appreciating the rich tapestry of her past that so graciously gifted her with the opportunity to birth her true potential.

She knows that the road ahead will always be paved with challenges but she has learnt that the light of inner guidance, the sword of truth and a heart of love will always conquer all. She recognises that achievement of any sort is a daily, steady endeavour towards a goal and that there is no such thing as indulging instant gratification on the path to success.

She honours the goddess in every woman as well as the many treasures that lie dormant within their souls, waiting to be claimed through their own recognition and self-love. She is committed to supporting every woman who seeks to embark on her own journey of re-discovery and her mission now is to inspire every female on the planet to her own greatness.

She would leave you with these final words for they stirred her soul and inspired her in her darkest moments. They speak of disengaging from the shadow of fear and making way for the light of true and everlasting potential, so that dreams may be realised. They speak of never fearing the sacrifices that need to be made in the face of accomplishing one's vision for she now knows that it's better to be afraid and give it one's best shot than to live with the deepest regret of never having tried.

"Our greatest fear is not that we are inadequate, our greatest fear is that we are powerful beyond measure. It is our light, not our darkness that most frightens us.

We ask ourselves: who am I to be brilliant, gorgeous, talented, and fabulous? Actually, who are you not to be? You are a child of God. Your playing small does not serve the world. There's nothing enlightened about shrinking so that other people won't feel insecure around you. We are all meant to shine, as children do. We were born to make manifest the glory of God that is within us. It's not just in some of us; it's in everyone and as we let our own light shine, we unconsciously give others permission to do the same. As we are liberated from our own fear, our presence automatically liberates others."

- Marianne Williamson -
(as quoted by Nelson Mandela in his inaugural speech)

Acknowledgements

Firstly, I would like to acknowledge YOU, the reader. Thank you for having the vision and the courage to embrace a new way of thinking about your life. I have no doubt that you will go on to create beauty and unconditional love for yourself and I salute you.

I thank the team who worked alongside me throughout the creation of this book - the KPI community, for your faith in me and for encouraging the birth of this book, and the team at Balboa Press for bringing it all to fruition. I also extend my greatest thanks to Kas, who has made so many of my business dreams possible, Judy my copy editor, Catherine my book designer and Andrew, the love of my life, for all your patience, love and assistance with the final stages of editing as well as the endless cups of tea.

Thank you so much for believing in me and my vision to bring healing, hope and empowerment to every woman who seeks the light and the goddess within.

About the Author

Desiree Marie Leedo is the founder of Invisible Goddess™ and a leading Divorce Recovery and Life Empowerment Specialist to women from all walks of life who seek to heal and create meaningful, self-fulfilled lives.

Drawing on her unique mix of over a decade's experience as a personal development and healing practitioner, she developed her cutting-edge six week process for moving from powerless to powerhouse, after the sudden and devastating breakup of her own 10-year marriage.

Today Desiree shares her inspiring philosophies and techniques with women who are committed to reclaiming their inner goddess, allowing them to dream, believe and achieve, so becoming the superstars of their own lives.

www.invisiblegoddess.com

Further Reading

Count Your Blessing by *Dr. John Demartini*

The Power is Within You by *Louise Hay*

The Power of Now by *Eckhart Tolle*

Women's Bodies, Women's Wisdom by
Dr. Christiane Northrup

Find your Strongest Life by *Marcus Buckingham*

How to Stop Worrying and Start Living by *Dale Carnegie*

Secrets of Attraction by *Sandra Anne Taylor*

Don't Divorce your Children by *Jennifer M. Lewis M.D. and
William A.H. Sammons M.D.*

Secrets About Life Every Woman Should Know by *Barbara
De Angelis*

The Right Questions by *Debbie Ford*

The Unmistakable Touch of Grace by *Cheryl Richardson*

Love & The Goddess by *Mary E. Coen*

Invisible Goddess
Additional Products

The following products are all part of a range of healing, uplifting and inspiring products in support of the processes contained within this book.

Diary & Life Planner

More than just a day-to-day diary, this beautifully illustrated Life Planner perfectly supports the Invisible Goddess process, helping you set goals for the year ahead in every area of your life, while also providing space for you to plan and review your weekly goals. Each week also begins with an inspiring new illustration and creation statement. This Diary & Life Planner is an essential tool for creating the life of your dreams.

Emotions & Gratitude Journal

This beautiful journal was created for you to be able to meet all your journalling needs as part of your daily Essential Self-Care programme. It has two distinct sections - one for emotional journalling and one for gratitude journalling. These activities are vital to keeping you connected to your own ideas, thoughts and desires while helping you to create a meaningful new life from a place of love and gratitude.

Workbooks & CD's

There are three separate workbook and CD packages that will help you to work through each phase of the Invisible Goddess process.

Each of these Workbook and CD packages require a 60-90 minute daily commitment and is delivered in the same format as if you were having a one-to-one session with Desiree herself. They include: short guided visualisations, suggested creation statements, theory, as well as step-by-step instruction for completing each daily exercise. Individual consultation time with Desiree, typically via Skype, is also available.

Phase One: Essential Self-Care Workbook & CD set

This set of Workbooks and CD's will help you to establish a daily routine and build a strong foundation for overcoming the initial trauma and shock following a breakup. At this stage It is vital to create a daily routine that will alleviate insomnia, regain physical vitality, move you out of emotional numbness and assist you in structuring your environment in a way that will propel you forward. This is a 7-day instruction, consisting of a 60-90 minute daily session which will effectively guide you through each step. This prepares you for the next phase of the process - Rapid Psychological Transformation.

Phase Two: Rapid Psychological Transformation Workbook & CD set

This set of Workbooks and CD's will help you overcome the deeper psychological issues surrounding your breakup like feelings of anger, resentment and fear. It allows you to make peace with where you are and what is happening while guiding you through completing an empowerment audit of every area of your life. This is a 14-day instruction, consisting of a 60-90 minute daily session. This phase of the process will move you out of the emotional rollercoaster stage and prepare you for the next phase of the process - the New Emerging You.

Phase Three: New Emerging You Workbook & CD set

This set of Workbooks and CD's will help you work through your self-esteem issues and show you how to set personal boundaries to protect the new life you are creating. Here we delve into every area of your life and create a new vision for the meaningful and self-fulfilled life you wish to create, along with an action plan for its attainment. This is a 21-day instruction, consisting of a 60-90 minute daily session and is suitable for every woman, married or divorced, single or in a relationship, who feels she is not living her full potential and wishes to introduce some changes or work towards creating a more meaningful and inspired life. This is a powerful package that will help any woman create the life of her dreams.

Additional uplifting, inspiring and practical new products that support women in their journeys of creating an empowered life are constantly being added to the product range. For more information or for purchases, please visit **www.invisiblegoddess.com**

Notes

Notes

Notes